Lean Bean Cuisine

Jay Solomon

Prima Publishing
P.O. Box 1260BK
Rocklin, CA 95677
(916) 632-4400

This book is dedicated to my brother and sister,
Gregory Solomon and Lisa Solomon.

Library of Congress Cataloging-in-Publication Data

Solomon, Jay
      Lean bean cuisine : over 100 tasty meatless
recipes from around the world / Jay Solomon.
        p.   cm.
      Includes index.
      ISBN 1-55958-438-6
      1. Cookery (Beans)   2. Vegetarian cookery.
      I. Title.
TX803.B4S64   1994   94-3862
641.6′ 565—dc20   CIP

97 **AA** 10 9 8 7 6

Printed in the United States of America

A note on nutritional data:
A per-serving nutritional breakdown of each recipe is given, rounded to the nearest whole number. If a range is given for the number of servings or the amount of an ingredient, the breakdown is based on an average of the figures given. Nutritional content may vary depending on the specific brands or types of ingredients used. "Optional" ingredients or those for which no specific amount is stated are not included in the breakdown.

Contents

Acknowledgments

Lean Bean Cuisine was inspired by an article I wrote for *Restaurants USA,* a highly respected trade publication. Jennifer Basye of Prima Publishing invited me to expand my culinary ideas into a cookbook, and I enthusiastically obliged.

This is my fourth cookbook, and over the years I have depended upon the valuable advice of a network of friends, family members, and students. I am lucky to have an all-star cast of "taste testers," including Emily Page Robin, Beth Ryan, Jessica Robin, Claire and Michele Terrelonge, Helena Das, and Tammy Livengood. Thanks also go to my long-time supporters Janet Welch, Roberto Dinero Cima, Shaun Carbunkley, James Paradiso, Allyson Bice, Adrienne Nims, Linda and Jon Meyerhoff, Freddi Pollack, and Jeff Lischer. Finally, my parents, Jesse and Ann Solomon, brother Gregory, sister Lisa, and my grandmother, Mary Badia Solomon, have all contributed feedback and anecdotes.

I received valuable information from the American Dry Bean Board, Idaho Bean Commission, California Dry Bean Advisory Board, and Kathleen Marron of World Variety Produce. Eden Foods generously provided a variety of beans and pantry staples. I took some of the recipes for a test drive at my cooking seminars at The Boston Center for Adult Education and at the Greenstar Cooperative Market in Ithaca, New York.

For many years I owned Jay's Cafe, a restaurant in Ithaca, where my version of bean cuisine has its origins. I may miss Jay's Cafe, but bean cuisine lives on.

Introduction

Welcome to the exciting new world of bean cookery. *Lean Bean Cuisine* is filled with high-spirited dishes infused with flair, panache, and extraordinary flavors. Today's bean cookery will pique your culinary curiosity and bring pleasure to your palate.

Beans are perfect for today's healthful lifestyle. The humble legumes are nutritional gems, easy to prepare, inexpensive, and widely available. Far from being a collection of humdrum recipes with a bowl-a-beans on every page, Lean Bean Cuisine features a vast array of adventurous, nourishing, and imaginative meals, including soups, salads, main entrees, side dishes, and breakfast fare. If you are looking for healthful food that tastes good, you've hit the jackpot.

The term "beans" loosely refers to the members of the legume family, which also includes split peas, lentils, and peanuts. They are pod-bearing plants that split open when mature, releasing the seeds. There are hundreds of varieties of legumes, from kidney-shaped red and white beans, oval black beans, and elliptical lentils to cream-colored black-eyed peas and brilliantly mottled anasazi and Jacob's cattle beans. Legumes come in a multitude of shapes, sizes, and colors.

For centuries, beans have played a universal role in food, from the shores of the Mediterranean to the islands of the Caribbean, from the American Southwest to South America, from Africa to Asia. The world's menu is full of beans: Italian *pasta e fagioli*, Indian *dal*, Cajun red beans and rice, Cuban black bean soup, Mexican refried beans, Native American *posole*, Brazilian *feijoada*, Middle Eastern hummus, and Boston baked beans are on the hit parade of international dishes. Beans are worldly.

Despite this historical and multicultural omnipresence, beans have not always enjoyed rave reviews within every culinary circle. In fact, not too long ago beans were on the verge of falling into an abyss of obsolete cuisine. Restaurants rarely featured beans on the menu. Refried beans were synonymous with indigestion. Three-bean salads spent their days loitering at salad bars, looking anemic and bored. Vegetarians appreciated beans, but so did high school cafeterias. Beans were on the outskirts of town and heading out.

That was then, this is now. Beans are on the rebound and have never been more popular. People are cooking and eating more healthful foods. Supermarkets and natural food stores are expanding shelf space and selling more and more varieties of beans. There is also a growing interest in ethnic cuisines, a traditional haven for bean-inspired dishes.

Many restaurant chefs have rediscovered the bean's culinary potential. At my restaurant, there was always a pot of beans soaking and another one slowly simmering on the stovetop. We even offered a bean of the day for discerning customers. Some trendy restaurants, of course, have anointed beans with the obligatory gourmet price tag. (When that happens, you know beans have hit the big time.)

The vegetarian movement, a veritable booster club for beans, is one of the largest factors contributing to the growing popularity of legumes. Vegetarian cuisine, once a fringe element in the culinary world, has blossomed into an exciting discipline with unlimited epicurean possibilities. As vegetarian tastes have hit the mainstream, more and more people have developed a renewed appetite for nourishing foods such as beans.

All of the recipes in this book are completely vegetarian. The traditional denizens of bean cookery—ham hocks, salt pork, bacon, and so forth—have been given their walking papers. And while beans are at center stage, they are surrounded by a dynamic supporting cast of vegetables, tubers, roots, grains, and pastas. In addition, a plethora of herbs, spices, and chile peppers enliven the show.

So if you are striving to eat healthful meals with delicious flavors, you've come to the right place. In this new world of bean cookery, beans are liberated from the antiquated dishes of the past and elevated to the deserving level of gourmet status. Bean cuisine is casual, but elegant. *Lean Bean Cuisine* offers proof that food that *tastes* good can also be good for you.

The Healthful Bean

Beans are a "power food," loaded with nutrients and fiber and low in fat, calories, and sodium. On the whole, beans provide a significant nutritional dividend in return for the calories acquired. Like all food derived from plants, beans have zero cholesterol.

Beans, peas, and lentils provide a mother lode of nutrients. They are high in vitamins and minerals, including the B-complex vitamins, iron, calcium, potassium, zinc, and magnesium. In addition, beans are the kingpin of protein in the vegetable world. (Although the protein is incomplete, when beans are served with rice, tortillas, bread, or other cereal grains, the protein is completed.) Additionally, beans are considered a good source of complex carbohydrates. They take a long time to digest, making you feel sated longer.

Although dried beans are naturally low in sodium, canned beans come with a bit more baggage. Rinsing the canned beans, however, dramatically reduces the sodium content. Recently, several versions of low-sodium canned beans have been showing up at the supermarkets. Eden Foods, for example, offers an excellent line of canned beans using kombu, an edible seaweed, in lieu of salt. You can also buy dry kombu for home preparation.

Beans, peas, and lentils are rich in dietary fiber. Also called roughage, fiber is the indigestible part of our food, which provides bulk and promotes regularity in our digestive system. There are two kinds of dietary fiber, insoluble and water soluble; beans supply both forms. For the record, insoluble fiber relieves constipation, and water-soluble fiber has been shown to decrease blood cholesterol levels.

This emphasis on eating well is not a fleeting fad. Every week, it seems, there is a new report linking a health-conscious diet with a reduced risk of coronary heart disease, cancer, and other maladies. Nutritionists consistently recommend a diet that is low in fat, cholesterol, and sodium and high in fiber, vitamins, and minerals. Given that, if this were a bingo game, legumes would have all the right letters.

National health organizations, including the National Cancer Institute and the Produce for a Better Health Foundation, have recently introduced the "5 a Day For a Better Health" campaign. This program's mission is to encourage people to eat five servings of fruits and vegetables a day while maintaining a high-fiber diet.

Toward that end, many of the recipes in *Lean Bean Cuisine* embrace the 5-a-Day objectives. You will find an abundance of ways to include vegetables, grains, pastas, and fruits in a well-balanced, high-fiber, and high-nutrient lifestyle. Butter and cream make infrequent appearances, and I have omitted fried dishes altogether. (Falafel and bean fritters, alas, are not on the guest list.)

The Basics of Bean Cookery

Beans require more attention and planning than the average kitchen staple. Beans aren't merely cooked; they are nurtured. Dry, dehydrated beans must be soaked and reconstituted before cooking (excluding lentils and split peas). Like homemade bread, beans gradually come to life, but they need coaxing and an occasional helping hand.

The first step is to sort through the beans and pick out any loose pebbles or sand. Spread the beans out in a shallow bowl and proceed as if you were sorting for broken shells in a bowl of walnuts. Inspect the beans with your fingers, and shake the dish as though you were panning for gold. After you are satisfied, rinse the beans in cold water. The beans are now ready to be soaked.

In a perfect world, you should soak the beans overnight in three to four times the volume of water. If time does not permit an overnight soaking, give the beans at least four hours of soaking to rehydrate them. Soaking reduces the cooking time and softens the beans. At the end of the soaking time, drain the liquid and cook the beans in fresh water.

Beans will double or triple in size, so soak them in a large pot or storage container. One cup of dried beans yields two to three cups of cooked beans. One pound of dried beans yields about six cups of cooked beans.

In addition to rehydration, soaking the beans serves another purpose. By discarding the soaking liquid, you partially remove the complex sugars—oligosaccharides—that cause indigestion and other gastric problems, nod, nod, wink, wink. (More on that later.) The sugars are leached out when you drain the beans. All your troubles go down the drain.

If you are short on time, or simply forgot to soak the beans in advance, there is an alternative to the "perfect world" soaking method. It is known as the quick soak method: Place the sorted beans and water in a saucepan and bring to a rolling boil. Simmer for 2 minutes and then remove from the heat. Allow the beans to sit for 1 to 2 hours. Discard the soaking water and then proceed with the cooking process.

One caveat to the quick soak method: the beans are often not as plump, and they require a longer cooking time. In addition, fewer complex sugars are removed during the process. There is another back-up plan: Stock a variety of canned beans in your pantry. That way, you'll always have cooked beans ready for reheating.

Once the beans have been sated with water and drained, they are ready for cooking. Combine the beans with three to four times their volume of fresh water in a saucepan and simmer over low heat. Do not cover the pan. Check the beans occasionally to make sure they are completely covered with water and the water hasn't evaporated too quickly. Add more hot water if necessary. Cook until the beans are tender or for the recommended cooking time.

Cooking times vary for each legume; the larger the bean, the more time is required. Lentils have the quickest cooking time, while fava beans, kidney beans, and chick peas need 2 to 3 hours of cooking. Also, the older the bean, the longer it takes to cook. The slower the beans cook, the easier they will be to digest.

To check the degree of doneness, remove a few beans from the pot with a slotted spoon and place on a flat surface. Press a fork or·spoon against a bean; it should mash easily. Beans destined for salads and sautéed dishes should be cooked until they are soft and tender but still retain their shape. Beans intended for sauces, soups, and stews do not require much fuss. Once cooked, the beans are ready to be included in the bean dish or refrigerated for later use.

It is important *not* to salt the beans during the cooking stage. Salt inhibits the absorption of liquid and should be added only when the beans have reached the desired stage of tenderness. Acidic ingredients, such as tomatoes and vinegar, also retard the cooking process, sometimes causing the beans to split. Once salt or tomato products have been added to the beans, the bean skin will not soften any further.

Although traditional bean cookery often calls for ham hocks, salt pork, or other meat by-products, I prefer to aggressively season the beans with herbs, spices, ginger, garlic, chile peppers, and sometimes vegetable stock. Dark beans, such as black, red kidney, and pinto beans, benefit from strong seasonings, such as cumin, cilantro, chile peppers, garlic, and chili powder. Light beans, such as great northern beans, white kidney beans, navy beans, and chick peas are enhanced by aromatic herbs and spices, such as tarragon, thyme, oregano, basil, and curry powder.

Choosing and Storing Beans

Shop for beans at markets where there is likely to be a high turnover. The older the bean, the longer it takes to cook. Beans should be whole, not cracked or chipped. Bright colors signify fresher beans. When the season permits, farmers' markets are great sources for beans.

Store your beans in airtight containers in a cool place. Remember to rotate the beans—use up the oldest beans first before diving into a new batch. Store any cooked beans in the refrigerator. Refrigerated beans will last for four to five days.

The Bane of Beans

Any in-depth discussion of beans must, of course, confront the issue of bean bloat. Poorly prepared beans may cause digestive problems for people not accustomed to eating high-fiber foods. The problem is not unique to beans—cabbage, carrots, and grapes trigger similar reactions. Still, for many people, the topic is specifically linked to beans, especially for those who eat beans infrequently. It's the bean thing.

There are ways to reduce the gastric distress associated with beans. As mentioned above, properly soaking, rinsing, and draining the beans before cooking leaches out many of the complex sugars responsible for bean bloat. Thoroughly cooking beans will also make them easier to digest.

If you are a newcomer to the bean routine, it is a good idea to gradually build up your body's tolerance level by eating small amounts of beans at first. By increasing your bean consumption in small increments over time, you'll develop the hardy digestive enzymes needed to absorb beans into your system. In addition, drinking plenty of liquids will enable your system to adjust better to the extra fiber.

Some legumes are more troublesome than others. Anasazi beans, adzuki beans, mung beans, and lentils are easier to digest than navy, kidney, and black beans. A Mexican herb, *epazote,* which is similar to cilantro, is said to help matters if it is added to the beans as they cook. Asian recipes often call for ginger and turmeric to ease the digestion.

There is a commercial product, a liquid additive called Beano, that advertises itself as an antidote for potential bean predicaments. When you add Beano to the beans right before eating them, it breaks down the sugars and enhances the beans' digestibility.

In the long run, the best approach is to eat beans on a regular basis and make beans a part of a well-balanced diet. And that's where this book comes in.

Lean Bean Cuisine features a variety of flavorful international recipes designed for today's healthful lifestyle. Beans add flavor, texture, and substance to a wide gamut of meals.

As consumers' craving for wholesome, nutritious "comfort" foods increases, interest in bean cuisine will continue to grow. With *Lean Bean Cuisine,* beans have finally won their independence from the tyranny of old stereotypes and are transformed into enlightened gourmet fare.

Glossary of Legumes

The world of beans is filled with versatile, multicolored, multishaped members. The membership appears to be growing, but what is really happening is that more kinds of beans are arriving at the marketplace. We are lucky to have the whole gamut of beans available. Stand in the bean aisle of your supermarket and take a look around, and you'll see what I mean. There has never been a better time in the world for beans.

Although legumes have an international resumé and are enjoyed throughout the world, many are grown right here in the United States. The states of Michigan, California, Idaho, Nebraska, Minnesota, and Colorado are among the major growers. In addition, more and more beans are appearing at local farmers' markets across the country.

This glossary is grouped into two sections: mainstream beans, which include lentils and split peas, and heirloom beans. Mainstream beans are legumes you will easily recognize and find readily available all over the country. Heirloom beans are ancient beans with stories to tell. The seeds have been passed from generation to generation, and are often more expensive (and harder to find) than mainstream beans (but worth the effort). For this reason, heirloom beans are sometimes called designer beans.

Mainstream Beans

Adzuki beans Also called azuki, aduki, and adsuki. Small, oval-shaped beans with a deep reddish burgundy color and a thin white line on their ridges, adzukis have a nutty, light flavor perfect for sweet and savory dishes, especially when crushed into a paste. Grown in Japan and China for centuries, their popularity is increasing here in the States. Available dried and canned in Asian markets, health food stores, and some supermarkets, they take 1 to 1½ hours to cook.

Black beans Also called turtle beans and *frijoles negros*. Medium-sized, oval-shaped beans with an earthy, woodsy flavor, black beans are prevalent in Latin America, the Caribbean, Brazil, Mexico, and South and Central America. They are available dried and canned in most grocery stores, and they take 1 to 1½ hours to cook. This is the star legume of Caribbean soups and Brazilian *feijoada*.

Black-eyed peas Also called black-eyed beans, black-eyed Suzies, crowder peas, and cow peas. Medium-sized, roundish beans with a two-creams-in-your-coffee color and a dark "eye" on their ridges, black-eyed peas are savory, earthy, and smooth-flavored. They are used in the American South, Africa, the Caribbean, India, and the Middle East. They are available dried, canned, and frozen in most supermarkets. They take 45 minutes to 1 hour to cook. Eating black-eyed peas on New Year's Eve or New Year's Day is a tradition in some parts of the world.

Chick peas Also called garbanzo beans and ceci beans, chick peas are medium to large in size, with a bulging, acorn shape and tiny peak. The tan, cream-colored beans have a chewy texture and nutty taste. They are used in the Mediterranean, India, the Caribbean, and the Middle East and are available dried and canned in most supermarkets. They take 1 to 2 hours to cook. Chick peas are a staple of the ancient Roman diet— Cicero took his name from the bean. This is also the bean of hummus fame.

Cow peas Also called brown crowder peas and Southern peas. Not to be confused with black-eyed peas, these are tiny, round beans with a brownish coffee color. They are available dried and canned in some supermarkets. They take about 1 hour to cook. Cow peas are interchangeable with pigeon peas.

Cranberry beans Also called roman beans, shelly beans, and tongues of fire. Small- to medium-sized, with a speckled, cranberry-colored skin, these beans turn solid pink when cooked. They are similar to pinto beans in flavor. They are used in Italy, Chile, and South America, and in Native American cooking and are available dried and fresh (in seasonal markets). They take about 45 minutes to cook. They are a farmers' market staple.

Fava beans   Also called broad beans, faba beans, and horse beans. Creamy brown with tough reddish brown skin, fava beans are available in both large and small varieties. They are a staple in European and Middle Eastern cooking. The smaller variety, common in Egyptian cooking, is used in *ful medames*. They need a long soaking time and take about 2 hours to cook.

Great northern beans   Also called haricot beans. These medium- to large-size white beans are similar to white cannelini beans. They are popular in French and Italian food and are available dried and canned in most supermarkets. They take 1 to 1½ hours to cook. Great northern beans are interchangeable with navy beans.

Lentils   There are a myriad of lentils—brown, green, red, yellow, and so on. Lentils have a narrow oval shape similar to a thin disc. They are prevalent in Indian, Middle Eastern, North African, and European cooking. Dried brown lentils are widely available. Red, green, and yellow lentils can be found in Indian and Asian markets and specialty food stores. They take about 45 minutes to cook. *Lens* is the Latin word for lentil, hence the name for the glass of that shape.

Small lima bean   Also called butter beans, baby limas, and calico beans. Actually the smaller cousin of the large lima, not a younger version, this thumbnail-shaped pale white bean has its roots in South America (Lima is Peru's capital) as well as Africa and Central America. They take about 1 hour to cook. They are available dried and canned in most supermarkets.

Large lima beans Also called *habas grandes, gigandes,* Burma, and Rangoon. Wide beans with a creamy white color and smooth, starchy flavor, similar to small limas, large limas take about 1½ hours to cook. They are available dried and canned in most supermarkets and are great for mopping up the garlicky Greek *skordalia* sauce.

Green Fordhook lima beans Not to be confused with dried white lima beans, these beans are green and available frozen and canned in most supermarkets. They take only about 10 minutes to cook.

Navy beans These are small, oval white beans that take their name from their prominent role in the U.S. Navy's meal plan. When recipes call for small white beans, they often mean this bean. They are available dried and canned in most supermarkets and take 1 to 1½ hours to cook. This is the bean of Boston baked bean fame and Senate navy bean soup.

Peanuts Also called ground nuts, goober peas, and earth nuts. The peanut is neither a pea nor a nut. Peanuts are legumes. The peanut plant produces tiny, pea-shaped flowers above the ground; after pollination, it buries the seed pods in the ground to ripen. Peanuts vary in size, but are usually a roundish oval. Tan and smooth, with an eponymous flavor, they are enjoyed all over the world, including the Caribbean, South America, Africa, Southeast Asia, and, of course, here in America. They are available everywhere and are the source of peanut butter, which is also called ground nut sauce.

Split peas Also called field peas. Split peas are green and yellow whole peas that have been split in half. When cooked, they lose their shape and meld together nicely. Split peas have a rustic, grassy flavor. They are prevalent in Mediterranean, European, Indian, and early American food and are available everywhere. Great for soups and porridge, they can sometimes be substituted for lentils.

Pigeon peas   Also called gungo peas, Congo peas, *gandules*. Small, roundish, brownish yellow beans with a tiny eye and faint freckles, pigeon peas are closely related to cow peas. They are available canned (and occasionally dried) in Hispanic markets and many grocery stores and take about 1 hour to cook. These beans are favored on many Caribbean islands, especially in gungo pea soup and rice and peas.

Pink beans   Also called pinquito beans. Oval-shaped, smaller than a kidney bean with a pale rose color, these are interchangeable with small red chili beans and pinto beans. They are available dried and canned in most grocery stores and take about 1 hour to cook.

Pinto beans   These mottled, pinkish brown, oval-shaped beans are rich and full-flavored. When cooked, the faint markings fade to pink. Native to the Americas, pinto beans are a staple of Mexican, Tex-Mex, and Southwestern food. They are available dried and canned everywhere and take about 1 hour to cook. This is the bean of choice for refried beans. Pinto means "painted"; they also share the markings of the pinto horse.

Red chili beans   Also called Mexican chili beans and *habas pequenas coloradas*. Small red beans with deep burgundy color and oval shape, these are available dried and canned in most supermarkets. They take 1 to 1½ hours to cook. Red chili beans are an acceptable substitute for black beans.

Lean Bean Cuisine

Red kidney beans Also called Mexican beans. This bean takes its name from its kidney-like shape. It is a rich, full-flavored bean with dark and light red hues. They are available dried and canned everywhere and take 1 to 1½ hours to cook. The red kidney bean is cousin to the cannelini, a white bean of the same shape. This is the preferred bean for chili, Jamaican red pea soup, and red beans and rice.

Soybeans Also called soya beans. Soybeans are the size of a large pea. Although only tan and yellow varieties are available in the States, soybeans come in black, green, brown, and red. They require an extremely long cooking time and are not commonly prepared in their natural bean form. Soybeans are most often processed into soy sauce, tamari, miso, soy milk, soy flour, tofu, tempeh, fermented bean pastes, and soybean oil. Many of these processed products are available in grocery stores. The Chinese first cultivated soybeans centuries ago.

White cannellini beans Also called white kidney beans and *haricots blanc*. These beans have a smooth texture and slightly nutty flavor. Popular in European cooking, especially Italy, they are available dried and canned in most supermarkets. They take 1 to 1½ hours to cook. These make a good "white" chili and stew.

Heirloom Beans

Heirloom beans were once hard to find, but nowadays many specialty food stores and natural food stores are stocking a dizzying array of varieties, all worth a taste. Here is an overview of some of the more notable "designer beans" making inroads into the bean bins of many stores.

When you find "new" beans, take them home and try them out in a recipe.

Anasazi beans This is one of my favorite beans. These slightly kidney-shaped beans with reddish purple skin and mottled, creamy white streaks were grown by the Anasazi Indians in Colorado and the American Southwest and are still sold at farmers' markets in that region. They take about 1 hour to cook.

Appaloosa beans Known for their blackish brown spots similar to Appaloosa ponies, these take about 1 to 1½ hours to cook.

Jacob's cattle beans These beans have white and purple mottled skin similar to anasazi beans. They retain their markings during the cooking process and take 1 to 1½ hours to cook.

Flageolet beans Not really an heirloom bean, but still hard to find. The immature kidney bean is pale green and kidney shaped with a tender skin. Popular in France and Italy, they have a delicate taste. They take 45 minutes to 1 hour to cook.

Christmas lima beans Also called calico, speckled lima, and speckled butter bean. These large, brownish and purplish mottled beans with roasted chestnut flavor take about 1½ hours to cook.

Calypso beans Kidney-shaped with stark black-and-white markings, these take 1 to1½ hours to cook.

Tepary beans This is an ancient Mexican bean favored by Southwestern chefs. It is a small, flat bean with multiple colors: white, tan, black, or gold. It retains its color after cooking and takes about 1 hour to cook.

European soldier beans Also called soldier beans. These beans have reddish brown marks on a white background, with a keel similar to a soldier caricature. They take 1 to 1½ hours to cook.

Savory Soups, Chilis, Chowders, and Stews

Some people relieve stress by eating chocolate. Others gorge on ice cream. For me, a hearty bean soup is the antidote. Give me a big bowl of bean soup and a hunk of fresh bread, and I'm on cloud nine. When the soup's on, all is well. A bean soup simmering on the stovetop fills the kitchen with warm, satisfying aromas and glowing expectations.

However, this wholesome, feel-good aura was not always the message conveyed by bean soups. To past generations, bean soups were equated with peasant food. Those were the days when beans were a cheap substitute for a "real meal" of meat and potatoes. No one walked around bragging about the bean soup they just made. Beans were valued more for their stick-to-your-ribs quality than for their culinary appeal.

How things change. Nowadays, beans provide the impetus for a limitless variety of nourishing soup-meals. From Jamaican Red Pea Soup to Southwestern Black Bean Soup, Rocky Mountain Chili with Anasazi Beans to Split Pea, Barley, and Rutabaga Stew, this chapter is filled with imaginative and hearty soups, chilis, chowders, and stews. There is a soup for every season, a tureen for every mood.

Soups are an excellent place for improvisation and to place your individual stamp on the meal. It doesn't take a culinary degree to make a great soup, just wholesome ingredients and a sense of taste and time. It is hard to overcook a bean soup. The longer the beans cook, the better the flavor and texture. Simmering and occasional stirring is the modus operandi here. It is a good idea to make large batches; most soups taste just as good or better when reheated the next day. When tightly wrapped, most bean soups also freeze well.

One key to expanding your bean soup repertoire is a well-stocked pantry of fresh herbs and spices. Variety is the spice of life, and a good spice rack gives life to soups. At my restaurant, I was spoiled by the luxury of having every spice from A to Z at my fingertips. With a plethora of seasonings, there is less inclination to reach for the salt or the heavy cream.

Jamaican Red Pea Soup

This soup is a full meal in a bowl. In Jamaica, red kidney beans are called "red peas." This soup is prepared in down-island fashion: Whole sprigs of fresh thyme and a whole Scotch bonnet pepper (the world's hottest) are simmered in the soup and removed at the end. Thyme gracefully seasons the soup, while the notoriously hot chile pepper contributes an aromatic heat. There's always a starch or squash of some kind, such as yam or calabaza (West Indian pumpkin) in this type of soup.

Two Jamaican friends, Claire and Michele Terrelonge, contributed to this recipe.

2   cups red kidney beans, soaked and drained
About 10 cups water
2   tablespoons vegetable oil
2   medium onions, diced
1   large green bell pepper, seeded and diced
3 or 4   cloves garlic, minced
1   fresh Scotch bonnet pepper
        or other whole hot chile pepper
4   scallions
1   large carrot, peeled and diced
1   cup diced yam, potato, or calabaza
        (found in Hispanic or Caribbean markets),
        or other winter squash
4 or 5   sprigs fresh thyme or 2 teaspoons
        dried thyme leaves
1   cup canned coconut milk
½   teaspoon ground allspice
½   teaspoon ground black pepper
1   teaspoon salt

Combine the beans and water in a saucepan and cook over medium heat for about 45 minutes. Drain, reserving 5 cups of the cooking liquid, and set aside.

Heat the oil in a saucepan and add the onion, bell pepper, and garlic. Sauté for 7 minutes, until the onion is tender.

Puncture the Scotch bonnet pepper with a fork and add to the pan. Add the beans, reserved cooking liquid, and all of the remaining ingredients except the salt. Bring to a simmer and cook for 1 to 1½ hours over low heat, stirring occasionally. Taste the soup periodically, and remove the pepper when it reaches the spice level you desire.

Before serving, remove the thyme and chile (if you haven't already). Stir in the salt, to taste, and serve hot. If there is a chile pepper connoisseur dining with you, give him or her the chile pepper.

Yield: 8 servings

Each serving provides:

292	Calories	41 g	Carbohydrate
13 g	Protein	299 mg	Sodium
10 g	Fat	0 mg	Cholesterol
7 g	Dietary Fiber		

Big Lentil Chili

Once you remove the vestiges of meat from the chili equation, a new gustatory horizon opens up. It becomes possible to include a wide range of legumes, vegetables, and seasonings. For this version, lentils and potatoes conspire to form a spicy, robust chili. It is the perfect antidote to a chilly afternoon.

2   tablespoons vegetable oil
1   medium onion, diced
1   red bell pepper, seeded and diced
2   carrots, peeled and diced
1   cup diced celery
2   cloves garlic, minced
1   jalapeño pepper, seeded and minced
2   cups dried brown lentils, soaked and drained
2   cups diced white potatoes
6   cups water
2   tablespoons chili powder
1   tablespoon dried oregano
½   tablespoon ground cumin
1 to 2   teaspoons Tabasco
      or other bottled hot sauce
½   teaspoon ground black pepper
½   teaspoon salt
1   can (16 ounces) whole tomatoes
1   can (15 ounces) crushed tomatoes

Heat the oil in a large saucepan and add the onion, bell pepper, carrot, celery, garlic, and jalapeño. Sauté for 7 minutes over medium heat.

Add the lentils, potatoes, water, and seasonings and cook for 20 minutes, stirring occasionally. Stir in both kinds of tomatoes, reduce the heat, and cook for 20 to 30 minutes more, until the potatoes and lentils are tender.

Ladle into soup bowls and serve topped with diced red onion, minced cilantro, or shredded provolone or Gouda cheese. Pinto Bean and Double Corn Bread (page 236) makes a nice accompaniment.

Yield: 8 servings

Each serving provides:

276	Calories	46	g	Carbohydrate
16 g	Protein	369	mg	Sodium
5 g	Fat	0	mg	Cholesterol
9 g	Dietary Fiber			

Black Bean and Tomato Gazpacho

Every gardener should have a gazpacho recipe in his or her culinary repertoire. Gazpacho is a chilled tomato and vegetable soup perfect for a hot summer day, especially at the peak of a summer's harvest. So when you are bent over weeding and your back aches, think of the gazpacho in your future. I prefer a chunky gazpacho with lots of vegetables and spices, as opposed to a dainty, brothy soup. The beans add additional sustenance and flavor. This ain't no sipping soup.

3 or 4   plum tomatoes, cored and chopped
1   small onion, diced
1   green or red bell pepper, seeded and diced
1   cucumber, peeled and chopped
1   small jalapeño or serrano pepper,
      seeded and minced
2   cloves garlic, minced
1   tablespoon minced fresh cilantro
1½ teaspoons ground cumin
1   teaspoon Tabasco or other bottled hot sauce
¼   teaspoon ground black pepper
¼   teaspoon salt
1¼ cups cooked or canned black beans, drained
2   cups canned tomato juice

Lean Bean Cuisine

Combine all of the ingredients, except the black beans and tomato juice, in a food processor fitted with a steel blade or in a blender. Process for 10 to 15 seconds, forming a vegetable mash. Transfer to a large bowl. Blend in the tomato juice and black beans and chill for 1 hour.

When ready to serve, stir the gazpacho and ladle into soup bowls. Garnish with a sprig of cilantro.

Yield: 4 servings

Each serving provides:

129	Calories	26 g	Carbohydrate
7 g	Protein	594 mg	Sodium
1 g	Fat	0 mg	Cholesterol
3 g	Dietary Fiber		

Variations:
Serve topped with plain yogurt and fresh chives.
Make it a full meal by adding about ½ cup of cooked bulgur or couscous to the soup.

Southwestern Black Bean Soup

This is one of my favorite things in the entire bean universe. There was never leftover black bean soup at my restaurant, because if it didn't sell out, I ate what was left. The flavors of the Southwest—cumin, chiles, and earthy herbs—enhance the strong, smoldering quality of the black beans.

For variation, spoon a dollop of light sour cream or crumbled feta cheese over the top, or serve with salsa or Cucumber Raita (page 208).

1½   cups dried black beans, soaked and drained
6   cups water
2   tablespoons vegetable oil
1   large onion, diced
1   green or red bell pepper, seeded and diced
½   cup chopped celery
3 or 4   cloves garlic, minced
1   jalapeño pepper, seeded and minced
2   carrots, peeled and diced
3   tablespoons dry sherry (optional)
2   tablespoons minced fresh parsley
2 to 3   teaspoons dried oregano
2   teaspoons ground cumin
1   teaspoon ground coriander
1   teaspoon dried thyme or
        1 tablespoon fresh thyme
½   teaspoon ground black pepper
½   cup canned crushed tomatoes
1   teaspoon salt
4   scallions, finely chopped

Place the beans and water in a saucepan and cook for about 45 minutes. Drain, reserving 4 cups of the cooking liquid, and set aside.

Heat the oil in a saucepan and add the onion, bell pepper, celery, garlic, and jalapeño. Sauté for 7 minutes over medium heat, until the vegetables are tender.

Add the carrots, beans, reserved cooking liquid, sherry, and all of the seasonings except the salt. Bring to a simmer and cook for about 20 minutes, stirring occasionally.

Stir in the crushed tomatoes and salt and cook for 10 to 15 minutes more. If you prefer a thick soup, puree half of the soup in a food processor fitted with the steel blade and return to the pan. Stir in the salt.

Ladle the soup into bowls and sprinkle the scallions over the top.

Yield: 6 servings

Each serving provides:

252	Calories	41 g	Carbohydrate
12 g	Protein	424 mg	Sodium
6 g	Fat	0 mg	Cholesterol
9 g	Dietary Fiber		

Tuscan Bean Soup
with Leafy Green Vegetables

The people of Tuscany are prodigious bean eaters, especially white beans and cranberry beans. A combination of leafy greens—kale, Swiss chard, and spinach—give this soup a nourishing spin.

    1   cup dried cannellini, cranberry, or navy beans,
            soaked and drained
   10   cups water
    2   tablespoons olive oil
    2   cups chopped leeks, well rinsed
    1   cup diced celery
    8   mushrooms, sliced
    4   cloves garlic, minced
    2   carrots, peeled and diced
    1   cup chopped white or red potatoes
    3   cups mixture of shredded kale, Swiss chard,
            and spinach
    3   tablespoons tomato paste
    1   tablespoon dried basil
    1   tablespoon dried oregano
    2   teaspoons dried sage
   ½   teaspoon salt
   ¼   teaspoon dried red pepper flakes
    2   tablespoons dry red wine

Place the beans and water in a large saucepan and cook for 1 hour, until the beans are tender. Drain, reserving 6 cups of the cooking liquid, and set aside.

Heat the oil in another large saucepan and add the leeks, celery, mushrooms, and garlic. Sauté for about 7 minutes. Add the beans, reserved cooking liquid, and remaining ingredients and simmer for 20 minutes, stirring occasionally.

Ladle the soup into bowls and season with salt at the table. Serve hot with Italian bread.

Yield: 6 servings

Each serving provides:

244	Calories	40 g	Carbohydrate
11 g	Protein	313 mg	Sodium
6 g	Fat	0 mg	Cholesterol
7 g	Dietary Fiber		

Variation:
Add pasta spirals, elbows, or shells to the soup along with the cooked beans.

Peach Mulligatawny
with Chick Peas

*Mulligatawny is a traditional brothy Indian soup prepared
with curry seasonings, vegetables, sometimes apples, and, uh,
chicken. Not here, though. With a little imagination, this soup
has been transformed into a meatless masterpiece. I prepare it
with peaches, summer squash, leafy vegetables, raisins, and
chick peas. The raisins plump up with flavor, providing a tasty
and colorful contrast to the chick peas. If you prefer, substitute
apples for the peaches.*

2	tablespoons vegetable oil
1	medium onion, diced
1	green pepper, seeded and diced
1	yellow summer squash, diced
1	cup diced celery
2 or 3	cloves garlic, minced
1	tablespoon minced fresh ginger root
1	jalapeño pepper, seeded and minced
2	tablespoons curry powder
1	tablespoon ground cumin
2	teaspoons ground coriander
1	teaspoon salt
¼	teaspoon ground turmeric
¼	teaspoon ground cloves
¼	teaspoon black pepper
3 or 4	peaches, pitted and chopped
2	cups canned or cooked chick peas, drained
5	cups water or vegetable stock
½	cup raisins
2	cups shredded leafy green vegetables such as Swiss chard, kale, or spinach

Heat the oil in a large saucepan and add the onion, bell pepper, squash, and celery. Sauté for 5 minutes over medium heat. Stir in the garlic, ginger, and jalapeño and sauté until the vegetables are tender. Add the seasonings and cook for 1 minute more, stirring frequently.

Add the peaches, chick peas, water, and raisins and cook for 40 minutes over medium-low heat, stirring occasionally. Stir in the leafy greens and cook for about 10 minutes more.

Ladle into soup bowls and serve hot.

Yield: 6 servings

Each serving provides:

218	Calories	36 g	Carbohydrate
6 g	Protein	524 mg	Sodium
7 g	Fat	0 mg	Cholesterol
7 g	Dietary Fiber		

Rocky Mountain Chili
with Anasazi Beans

Although any red or pink bean will make a hearty chili, I like to use anasazi beans. They are freckled legumes common in native American cooking and very similar to cranberry beans, a staple among the native South Americans. I found fresh anasazi beans at a farmers' market in Colorado, along with an abundance of chiles, tomatoes, sweet peppers, onions, and chili powder. Soon afterward, this delicious bean chili was in the works.

1	cup anasazi beans or red kidney, cranberry, or pink beans, soaked and drained
2	tablespoons vegetable oil
1	medium onion, diced
1	red bell pepper, seeded and diced
1	cup chopped eggplant or summer squash
1	large carrot, peeled and diced
2	cloves garlic, minced
1	hot chile pepper, seeded and minced
1	large potato, diced (do not peel)
1	can (28 ounces) crushed tomatoes
2	tablespoons sugar
2	tablespoons chili powder
2	tablespoons dried oregano
1	tablespoon ground cumin
1 to 2	teaspoons Tabasco or other bottled hot sauce
2	teaspoons dried thyme
¼	teaspoon ground black pepper
¼	teaspoon salt

Place the beans in plenty of water to cover in a saucepan and cook for 1 hour. Drain, reserving 1½ cups of the cooking liquid, and set aside.

Heat the oil in a large saucepan and add the onion, bell pepper, eggplant, carrot, garlic, and chile. Sauté for 7 minutes over medium heat.

Add the beans, reserved cooking liquid, potato, crushed tomatoes, sugar, and seasonings and cook for about 40 minutes over medium-low heat, stirring occasionally.

Ladle into soup bowls and serve topped with shredded Colby or Havarti cheese and diced red onion.

Yield: 8 servings

Each serving provides:

195	Calories	33 g	Carbohydrate
8 g	Protein	288 mg	Sodium
5 g	Fat	0 mg	Cholesterol
5 g	Dietary Fiber		

New Mexican
Succotash Chowder

This was one of the most popular soups at my restaurant. It was inspired by the delectable combination of corn and lima beans. This hearty soup is spiced with the elegant New Mexico chile pepper, the curvaceous pod used in holiday ristras. Fresh New Mexico chiles are similar to Anaheim peppers, with a mild heat and fruity undertones. The peppers should first be roasted over a fire or beneath a broiler so that the tough outside skin can be removed. You can substitute Anaheim peppers.

For the roux:
2 tablespoons melted butter
2 tablespoons all-purpose flour

For the soup:
2 tablespoons vegetable oil
1 large Spanish onion, diced
1 large green or red bell pepper, seeded and diced
1 cup diced celery
2 to 3 cloves garlic, minced
1 fresh New Mexico chile pepper, roasted,
     peeled, seeded, and minced
4 to 5 cups water or vegetable stock
3 cups coarsely chopped sweet potatoes (unpeeled)
1 tablespoon paprika
1 tablespoon ground cumin
1 tablespoon dried oregano
1 tablespoon dried thyme
½ teaspoon salt
¼ teaspoon ground black pepper
2 cups Green Fordhook lima beans,
     frozen or canned, drained

2   cups corn kernels, fresh, frozen, or canned
3   cups milk or light cream

To make the roux, melt the butter in a skillet over medium heat. Gradually whisk in the flour, forming a paste. Cook for 5 minutes, stirring frequently. Remove from the heat and set aside.

Heat the oil in a large saucepan and add the onion, bell pepper, celery, garlic, and chile pepper. Sauté over medium heat for 7 to 10 minutes, until the vegetables are tender. Add the water, potatoes, and seasonings and simmer over medium heat for about 20 minutes, until the potatoes are easily pierced with a fork. Add the lima beans, corn, and milk and return to a low simmer for about 10 minutes, stirring occasionally. Whisk in the roux and cook for a few minutes more.

Ladle into soup bowls and serve hot. Season with salt at the table.

Yield: 8 servings

Each serving provides:

281	Calories	41	g	Carbohydrate
9	g Protein	267	mg	Sodium
11	g Fat	21	mg	Cholesterol
9	g Dietary Fiber			

Variation:
If New Mexico chile peppers are unavailable, try a small jalapeño.

Saint Lucian Pumpkin and White Bean Soup

In the Caribbean, the West Indian pumpkin (also called calabaza) is a large, watermelon-shaped squash with green or orange streaks and vivid orange flesh. When combined with beans, it is a popular soup staple on many islands, especially on Saint Lucia, where I first tasted this recipe.

Calabaza can be found in many Latin American markets. Butternut, red kuri, or acorn squash make acceptable substitutes, and you can even use the familiar jack-o'-lantern. Peel the squash, remove the seeds, and chop.

2	tablespoons vegetable oil
1	medium onion, diced
1	cup diced celery
2	cloves garlic, minced
1	jalapeño pepper
	or half a Scotch bonnet pepper, seeded and minced
1	tablespoon minced fresh ginger root
4	cups peeled, diced calabaza
	(West Indian pumpkin) or other winter squash
2	tablespoons minced fresh parsley
1	tablespoon fresh thyme leaves,
	or 1 teaspoon dried thyme
1	tablespoon curry powder
1	teaspoon ground cumin
½	teaspoon salt
½	teaspoon ground allspice
6	cups water or vegetable stock
1	cup chopped kale or spinach
1½	cups cooked or canned navy beans
	or other small white beans, drained

Heat the oil in a large saucepan and add the onion, celery, garlic, chile pepper, and ginger. Sauté over medium heat for about 7 minutes. Add the pumpkin and sauté for 3 minutes. Add the seasonings and sauté for 1 minute more. Add the water and simmer for about 20 minutes, stirring occasionally.

Stir in the kale and white beans and cook for another 10 to 15 minutes. Ladle the soup into bowls and serve hot.

Yield: 8 to 10 servings

Each serving provides:

108	Calories	17 g	Carbohydrate
4 g	Protein	139 mg	Sodium
3 g	Fat	0 mg	Cholesterol
2 g	Dietary Fiber		

Vegetable, Tortellini, and Kidney Bean Soup

Sometimes I crave a nourishing vegetable and bean soup and a loaf of freshly baked bread and nothing else. Put me in a room with a view and I'm satisfied. This soup inspires a wistful, contented mood. It's so good I can feel the nutrients coursing through my veins while I eat.

2 tablespoons vegetable oil
1 medium onion, diced
1 cup diced celery
1 green bell pepper, seeded and diced
1 small zucchini, diced
1 large tomato, cored and diced
8 to 12 mushrooms, sliced
2 cups cooked or canned red kidney
   or cannellini beans, drained
1 can (28 ounces) crushed tomatoes
4 cups water or vegetable stock
2 tablespoons fresh minced parsley
2 tablespoons dried basil
1 tablespoon dried oregano
1 teaspoon dried thyme
1 teaspoon ground black pepper
½ teaspoon salt
4 ounces cheese tortellini, refrigerated or frozen

Heat the oil in a large saucepan and add the onion, celery, bell pepper, zucchini, fresh tomato, and mushrooms. Cook over medium heat for 7 to 10 minutes, stirring occasionally. Add the beans, crushed tomatoes, water, and seasonings, reduce the heat, and cook for 15 minutes, stirring occasionally. Add the tortellini and cook for 15 to 25 minutes longer.

Ladle the soup into bowls and serve hot.

Yield: 8 servings

Each serving provides:

179	Calories	28 g	Carbohydrate
9 g	Protein	381 mg	Sodium
5 g	Fat	8 mg	Cholesterol
4 g	Dietary Fiber		

Variations:
Top with grated Parmesan or Romano cheese.
Stir in shredded kale or mustard greens along with the beans.
Add corn kernels or green peas.

Split Pea, Barley, and Rutabaga Stew

Split peas tend to lose their form when cooked for a long period of time, a habit that is perfect for soup. Here the peas are teamed with hearty barley and rutabaga, a vastly underrated vegetable. Even though the rutabaga looks like a prehistoric tuber transported through a time machine, it really can swing with today's hip beans and vegetables if given a chance.

2	tablespoons vegetable oil
1	medium onion, diced
2	carrots, peeled and chopped
1	cup diced celery
2 or 3	cloves garlic, minced
1	chipotle pepper or other dried chile pepper, soaked, seeded, and minced
10	cups water
1	cup dried split peas
2	cups peeled, diced rutabaga or turnip
½	cup barley
1	tablespoon ground coriander
1	tablespoon ground cumin
1	tablespoon dried oregano
1	teaspoon dried thyme
½	teaspoon ground black pepper
½	teaspoon salt

Heat the oil in a large saucepan and add the onion, carrot, celery, garlic, and dried chile pepper. Sauté over medium heat for 7 to 10 minutes, until the vegetables are tender, stirring occasionally. Add the water, peas, rutabaga, barley, and seasonings (except the salt) and simmer over medium-low heat for about 1 hour or more. Stir the soup occasionally.

When the soup reaches the desired thickness, season with salt and ladle into soup bowls. Serve hot.

Yield: 6 servings

Each serving provides:

258	Calories	42 g	Carbohydrate
12 g	Protein	228 mg	Sodium
6 g	Fat	0 mg	Cholesterol
7 g	Dietary Fiber		

Variation:
Try quinoa or coarse bulgur in place of the barley.

Pesto Navy Bean Soup with Red Bell Peppers

This is not, repeat, not, the hallowed Senate navy bean soup fraught with salt pork, bacon, and ham hocks. Rather, this is a refreshing break from tradition. Pesto, a garlicky paste of fresh basil, nuts, and cheese, adds a spectrum of flavors to this white bean soup. The red bell peppers add a splash of color.

2   cups navy beans or other small white beans, soaked and drained
About 10 cups water
2   tablespoons vegetable oil
2 or 3   red bell peppers, seeded and diced
1   medium onion, diced
1   yellow summer squash or zucchini, chopped
1   cup diced celery
½   teaspoon ground black pepper
¾   cup commercial or homemade pesto (page 100)
1   cup milk or soy milk
1   tablespoon cornstarch

Combine the beans and water in a saucepan and cook over medium heat for about 45 minutes. Drain, reserving 4 cups of the cooking liquid, and set aside.

Heat the oil in a large saucepan and add the peppers, onion, squash, and celery. Sauté for 7 to 10 minutes over medium heat.

Add the beans, reserved cooking liquid, and ground pepper and cook for about 30 minutes, stirring occasionally. Stir in the pesto and milk and bring to a simmer. Combine the cornstarch with 1 tablespoon of warm water and whisk into the soup. Simmer for 5 to 10 minutes more, stirring occasionally.

Ladle into bowls and serve hot with French bread.

Yield: 6 servings

Each serving provides:

481	Calories	54 g	Carbohydrate
20 g	Protein	229 mg	Sodium
22 g	Fat	10 mg	Cholesterol
8 g	Dietary Fiber		

Cajun Gumbo with Black-Eyed Peas

Gumbo is a hearty Cajun soup of okra and other vegetables seasoned with herbs and hot spices. Although traditional gumbo contains meat, you won't miss it in this meatless adaptation.

Gumbo filé is often used as a natural thickener for gumbos. It is made with ground sassafras leaves and has a grassy aroma. If you can't find gumbo filé, roux will suffice as a thickener (use the roux from New Mexican Succotash Chowder, page 34). Whisk it into the gumbo near the finish.

1	cup dried black-eyed peas, soaked and drained
8	cups water
2	tablespoons vegetable oil
1	large onion, diced
1	large green or red bell pepper, seeded and diced
1	cup diced celery
4	cloves garlic, minced
2	large tomatoes, cored and diced
2	tablespoons minced fresh parsley
1	tablespoon gumbo filé powder
2	teaspoons dried oregano
2	teaspoons sweet paprika
1	teaspoon dried thyme
½	teaspoon ground black pepper
½	teaspoon salt
¼	teaspoon cayenne
½	cup canned tomato puree
2	carrots, peeled and chopped
1½	cups chopped okra, thawed if frozen
½	cup uncooked brown rice

Place the peas and water in a large saucepan and cook for about 45 minutes. Drain, reserving 6 cups of the liquid, and set aside.

Heat the oil in another saucepan and add the onion, bell pepper, celery, and garlic. Sauté for 8 to 10 minutes, until the vegetables are tender. Add the tomatoes and seasonings and cook for another 7 minutes. Add the peas, reserved cooking liquid, and the remaining ingredients and simmer over low heat for 30 to 40 minutes, stirring occasionally.

Ladle the gumbo into bowls and season with Tabasco or other bottled hot sauce at the table. Serve hot with corn bread.

Yield: 6 servings

Each serving provides:

265	Calories	45 g	Carbohydrates
10 g	Protein	306 mg	Sodium
6 g	Fat	0 mg	Cholesterol
12 g	Dietary Fiber		

Watermargin Mixed Bean Hot Pot

Some of my best college memories occurred at place called Watermargin, a housing cooperative at Cornell University. As kitchen steward, I coordinated the meals for my 22 housemates. The soup du jour was whatever we could find in the pantry. These impromptu soups often turned into culinary masterpieces. Of course, nothing was ever written down, so this recipe is a general guide with several options along the way. Follow it and create your own pantry hot pot!

2   cups mixed dried beans, lentils, and split peas, soaked and drained
About 12 cups water
2   tablespoons vegetable oil
1   large red onion, diced
1   large green or red bell pepper, seeded and diced
1   cup diced celery
4 to 6   cloves garlic, minced
1   jalapeño pepper, seeded and minced
2   carrots, peeled and cut in ¾-inch pieces
2   cups peeled, diced winter squash
        or sweet potatoes
½   cup barley, brown rice, or quinoa
¼   cup dry sherry
2 to 3   tablespoons minced fresh parsley
1½ tablespoons dried oregano
1   tablespoon chili powder
2   teaspoons dried thyme
1   teaspoon ground black pepper
1   teaspoon salt
2   cups shredded kale, spinach, or escarole lettuce

Lean Bean Cuisine

Place the beans and water in a large saucepan and cook for 45 minutes. Drain, reserving about 8 cups of the liquid, and set aside.

In another large saucepan, heat the oil and add the onion, bell pepper, and celery and sauté for about 4 minutes. Add the garlic and chile and cook for 5 minutes more over medium heat.

Add the legumes, reserved cooking liquid, carrots, squash, barley, sherry, parsley, and seasonings (except the salt) and cook for 1 to 1½ hours over low heat, stirring occasionally. Stir in the salt and kale and cook 10 minutes more.

Ladle the soup into bowls. Serve with French bread and good company.

Yield: 8 to 10 servings

Each serving provides:

262	Calories	45 g	Carbohydrate
15 g	Protein	289 mg	Sodium
4 g	Fat	0 mg	Cholesterol
9 g	Dietary Fiber		

Bajan Gungo Pea
and Coconut Soup

*Some people travel to the Caribbean in pursuit of a beach tan
and relaxation. I, on the other hand, travel in search of
adventurous food. While on one of my culinary missions to
Barbados, I discovered this savory soup. It is made with
pigeon peas, which are called gungo peas in Barbados. This
soup features many characteristic flavors of the Caribbean,
including calabaza (West Indian pumpkin), fiery red peppers
(habaneros), coconut milk, rum, and fresh herbs. Butternut or
acorn squash can be substituted for the calabaza, and jalapeño
makes a mild fill-in for habanero.*

2   tablespoons vegetable oil
1   medium onion, diced
1   large carrot, peeled and diced
½   cup chopped celery
2   cloves garlic, minced
½ to 1   teaspoon minced habanero
         or jalapeño pepper
2   cups canned or cooked pigeon peas
         (gungo peas), drained
4   cups water or vegetable stock
1   cup peeled, diced winter squash
         (calabaza, butternut, or acorn)
2   tablespoons dark rum
1   tablespoon minced fresh parsley
1   tablespoon dried thyme (or 2 tablespoons fresh)
½   teaspoon ground black pepper
½   teaspoon salt
1   cup canned coconut milk

Heat the oil in a large saucepan and add the onion, carrot, celery, garlic, and chile pepper. Sauté for 7 minutes over medium heat, until the vegetables are tender.

Add the beans, water, squash, rum, parsley, and seasonings. Bring to a simmer and cook for 35 to 40 minutes, stirring occasionally. Add a little hot water or rum if the soup is too thick, or continue to simmer if it is too thin.

Stir in the coconut milk and return to a simmer. Transfer the soup to a food processor fitted with a steel blade and process for 15 seconds, until smooth. Ladle into soup bowls and serve hot.

Yield: 6 to 8 servings

Each serving provides:

192	Calories	18 g	Carbohydrate
5 g	Protein	177 mg	Sodium
11 g	Fat	0 mg	Cholesterol
4 g	Dietary Fiber		

Native American Posole

Sante Fe is where I savored my first bowl of posole, a savory corn and bean stew rooted in Native American and New Mexican cuisines. The meal is prepared with dried corn kernels, also known as hominy. When hominy is cooked, it has a chewy texture. Hominy can be found canned or frozen in most supermarkets. (If you are using dried hominy, cook the kernels in water for about 3 hours first.) Posole is traditionally prepared with meat, but that's where the beans come in.

Chipotle chiles give this dish a subtle, smoky heat. If you can't find chipotles and still want heat, try a fresh jalapeño.

1 or 2	chipotle peppers
2	tablespoons vegetable oil
1	medium onion, diced
1	red or green bell pepper, seeded and diced
1	small zucchini, diced
1	large tomato, cored and diced
2	cloves garlic, minced
2	cups cooked or canned white or yellow hominy
1	cup cooked or canned pink, pinto, or cranberry beans, drained
3	cups water or vegetable stock
2½	tablespoons tomato paste
2	teaspoons paprika
1½	teaspoons dried oregano
½	teaspoon ground black pepper
½	teaspoon salt

Soak the chipotle in warm water for 30 minutes. Drain the liquid, remove the seeds, and mince.

Heat the oil in a large saucepan and add the vegetables, garlic, and chipotle. Sauté for 6 to 8 minutes, until the vegetables are tender. Add the hominy, beans, water, tomato paste, and seasonings and simmer for 45 minutes to 1 hour, stirring occasionally.

Ladle the posole into soup bowls and serve with warm flour tortillas.

Yield: 4 servings

Each serving provides:

243	Calories	38 g	Carbohydrate
7 g	Protein	362 mg	Sodium
8 g	Fat	0 mg	Cholesterol
4 g	Dietary Fiber		

West African Ground Nut Stew

This thick, nutty stew is a staple in many African kitchens.

I prefer to use natural, unsweetened peanut butter for this recipe. If your natural peanut butter has separated during storage (the oil has risen to the top), stir it vigorously before using.

2   tablespoons vegetable oil
1   medium onion, diced
2   cloves garlic, minced
1   tablespoon minced fresh ginger root
2   medium potatoes, diced (about 2 cups)
6   cups water
2   cups unsweetened chunky peanut butter
¼   cup canned crushed tomato
1   cup shredded kale or spinach
½   cup chopped okra, thawed if frozen
2   teaspoons dried thyme
2   teaspoons ground cumin
1   teaspoon ground black pepper
½   teaspoon salt

Heat the oil in a large saucepan and add the onion, garlic, and ginger. Sauté for 5 to 7 minutes. Add the potatoes and water and cook for 15 to 20 minutes over medium heat, until the potatoes are tender. Add the peanut butter, crushed tomato, kale, okra, and seasonings and bring to a simmer, stirring frequently. If the peanut butter clumps together, whisk the mixture.

Ladle into soup bowls and serve hot.

Yield: 8 servings

Each serving provides:

481	Calories	23 g	Carbohydrate
18 g	Protein	407 mg	Sodium
36 g	Fat	0 mg	Cholesterol
2 g	Dietary Fiber		

Swirly White Bean and Beet Soup

This splendid soup requires an extra effort, but the result is well worth it. It is really two soups served in one bowl. The mild-mannered white bean soup contrasts with the brilliant purple soup derived from beets. Together, the soups are swirled into a New World–style borscht.

For the white bean soup:
1   cup dried navy beans
      or other small white beans, soaked and drained
4   cups water
1   small onion, diced
2   cloves garlic, minced
2   tablespoons dry white wine
¼   teaspoon ground white pepper

For the beet soup:
2   tablespoons vegetable oil
1   small onion, diced
3   cups diced fresh beets
3   cups water
2   tablespoons minced fresh parsley
1   teaspoon dried thyme
½   teaspoon ground black pepper
½   teaspoon salt
3 to 4   tablespoons minced fresh chives or scallions

Combine all of the ingredients for the white bean soup in a saucepan and cook for about 1 hour, until the beans are tender, stirring occasionally. Transfer the beans to a food processor fitted with a steel blade and process for 15 seconds, until smooth. Return to the saucepan and keep warm.

Meanwhile, make the beet soup: Heat the oil in another saucepan and add the onion. Sauté for 7 minutes over medium heat, until the onion is tender. Add the beets, water, and seasonings (except the chives) and cook for about 30 minutes, stirring occasionally, until the beets are easily pierced with a fork. Transfer the beet mixture to a food processor fitted with a steel blade and process for 15 seconds, until smooth. Return to the saucepan and keep warm.

When you are ready to serve the soup, ladle the white bean soup into bowls until half full. Fill up the bowls with the beet soup. Season with salt, swirl with a spoon, and top with the chives. Serve at once.

Yield: 6 servings

Each serving provides:

204	Calories	32 g	Carbohydrate
9 g	Protein	238 mg	Sodium
5 g	Fat	0 mg	Cholesterol
5 g	Dietary Fiber		

Ann's Pasta Fazool

Pasta fazool (the official title is pasta e fagioli) *is a serious Italian soup-meal, a chunky cornucopia of vegetable and herbal flavors. My mother made this nourishing soup on Sundays when I was growing up. The soup changed slightly from week to week, depending on everyone's mood and the season.*

1   cup dried navy beans
      or other small white beans, soaked and drained
7 to 8   cups water
2   tablespoons olive oil
1   medium onion, diced
1   cup diced zucchini
1   cup diced celery
8   mushrooms, sliced
2   cloves garlic, minced
3   plum tomatoes, coarsely chopped
1   white potato,
      scrubbed and cut into ¾ -inch pieces
1   large carrot, coarsely chopped
1   tablespoon dried basil
1   tablespoon dried oregano
1   teaspoon salt
¼   teaspoon dried red pepper flakes
1   cup uncooked pasta elbows, spirals, or shells
3   tablespoons tomato paste
¼ to ½   cup grated Parmesan cheese

Combine the beans and water in a stockpot and cook for 1 hour, until the beans are tender. Drain, reserving 5 cups of the cooking liquid, and set aside.

Heat the oil in a large saucepan and add the onion, zucchini, celery, mushrooms, and garlic. Sauté for 7 minutes. Add the tomatoes, potato, carrot, beans, reserved cooking liquid, and dried seasonings and simmer for 15 to 20 minutes. Stir in the pasta and tomato paste and simmer for another 15 to 20 minutes, until the pasta is al dente. Ladle into soup bowls and sprinkle with the cheese. Serve with Italian bread.

Yield: 4 to 6 servings

Each serving provides:

376	Calories	60 g	Carbohydrate
18 g	Protein	674 mg	Sodium
9 g	Fat	5 mg	Cholesterol
8 g	Dietary Fiber		

Variations:
Add fresh rosemary, basil, or thyme.
Substitute cranberry beans or chick peas for white beans.
Add a couple of tablespoons of dry red wine or sherry while the soup simmers.

Lentil and Pearl Barley Soup with Turnips

This robust soup is a welcome antidote for the winter blues. The recipe makes a large batch, but it is even better when reheated the next day.

2	tablespoons vegetable oil
1	medium onion, diced
1	red or green bell pepper, seeded and diced
1	cup diced celery
2	cloves garlic, minced
6 to 7	cups water or vegetable stock
2	cups diced turnips or all-purpose potatoes
1	cup dried lentils
½	cup pearl barley
2	carrots, peeled and diced
2	tablespoons dried or fresh minced parsley
1	tablespoon dried oregano
2	teaspoons dried thyme
1½	teaspoons dried sage
½	teaspoon ground black pepper
2	cups canned crushed tomatoes
2	tablespoons dry red wine
½	teaspoon salt

Heat the oil in a large saucepan and add the onion, bell pepper, celery, and garlic. Sauté for 7 minutes.

Add the water, turnips, lentils, barley, carrots, and seasonings (except the salt) and cook for 20 minutes over medium-low heat, stirring occasionally. Stir in the crushed tomatoes and wine and cook for 20 to 30 minutes more, until the lentils and barley are tender.

Ladle into soup bowls and serve hot. Season with salt at the table.

Yield: 8 servings

Each serving provides:

202	Calories	34 g	Carbohydrate
10 g	Protein	281 mg	Sodium
4 g	Fat	0 mg	Cholesterol
7 g	Dietary Fiber		

Sweet Potato, Leek, and White Bean Chowder

There is a kind of magic chemistry between potatoes, leeks, and beans. When they are sitting by themselves in a room, alone, let's say, they don't really command much attention. They are sort of nondescript. But when these humble ingredients are combined in a soup pot and allowed to cook and meld together, they form a savory, wondrous union. They create extraordinary flavors without a lot of fanfare.

1	cup dried white cannellini beans or large lima beans, soaked and drained
6	cups water
2	tablespoons vegetable oil
2	cups coarsely chopped leeks, well rinsed
2	carrots, peeled and diced
1	cup diced celery
2 or 3	cloves garlic, minced
2	cups diced sweet potatoes (do not peel)
1	teaspoon dried thyme
1	teaspoon ground white pepper
1	teaspoon salt
2	cups milk or light cream
1½	cups corn kernels, fresh, frozen, or canned
2	tablespoons minced fresh dill or tarragon (or 1 tablespoon dried)

Place the beans and water in a large saucepan and cook for 1 hour. Drain, reserving 4 cups of the cooking liquid, and set aside.

In another large saucepan, heat the oil and add the leeks, carrots, celery, and garlic. Sauté over medium heat for 7 to 10 minutes, until the vegetables are tender. Add the beans, reserved cooking liquid, sweet potatoes, and seasonings and bring to a simmer. Cook for about 20 minutes, until the potatoes are easily pierced with a fork. Add the milk, corn, and dill and return to a simmer, stirring occasionally.

Remove the chowder from the heat and ladle into bowls. Serve hot.

Yield: 4 to 6 servings

Each serving provides:

294	Calories		45 g	Carbohydrate
10 g	Protein		544 mg	Sodium
10 g	Fat		14 mg	Cholesterol
8 g	Dietary Fiber			

Variation:
For a thick chowder, whisk in a roux (see New Mexican Succotash Chowder, page 34) while the soup simmers.

Black Bean Chili with Red Kuri Squash

Black beans prove their versatility in this robust offering.

Red kuri squash is an up-and-coming member of the squash family with a thin skin and bright orange flesh. Any winter squash may be substituted.

1	cup dried black beans, soaked and drained
2	cups peeled, diced red kuri or butternut squash
1½	tablespoons vegetable oil
1	medium onion, diced
1	red bell pepper, seeded and diced
1	cup sliced celery
2	cloves garlic, minced
1	can (28 ounces) crushed tomatoes
2	tablespoons chili powder
2	tablespoons fresh minced parsley (or 1 tablespoon dried)
1	tablespoon ground cumin
2	teaspoons paprika
1 to 2	teaspoons Tabasco or other bottled hot sauce
½	teaspoon ground black pepper
½	teaspoon salt

Place the beans in plenty of water to cover in a saucepan and cook over low heat for about 1 hour. Drain, discarding the liquid.

Meanwhile, place the squash in another saucepan and cover with boiling water. Cook for about 10 minutes and drain. Let the squash cool slightly.

In a large saucepan, heat the oil and add the onion, bell pepper, celery, and garlic. Sauté for 7 minutes over medium heat.

Add the beans, squash, crushed tomatoes, and seasonings and cook for about 40 minutes over medium-low heat, stirring occasionally.

Ladle the chili into bowls and serve topped with shredded Colby or Havarti cheese and diced red onion.

Yield: 4 to 6 servings

Each serving provides:

266	Calories	46	g	Carbohydrate
12	g Protein	548	mg	Sodium
6	g Fat	0	mg	Cholesterol
10	g Dietary Fiber			

Jay's All-Purpose Vegetable Stock

Vegetable stocks are easy to make. Simply coarsely chop a variety of vegetables and herbs, cover with water, simmer for 1 to 2 hours, and then strain to remove the pulp. The resulting broth is potent and aromatic. The recipe below is just one combination of vegetables. Try other blends at your whim.

For an economical kitchen coup, you can also use your leftover vegetable trimmings, such as onion skins, carrot peels, celery ends, broccoli stalks, bell pepper ribs, kale or Swiss chard stems, herb branches, and so forth. Save your trimmings in the freezer until you can fill a whole pot. Then proceed with the stock recipe.

Use the vegetable stock in place of chicken or beef stock or in place of water when you are making soup with canned beans. Or when you want to give a soup or sauce a deep vegetable flavor, blend it with the bean liquid (the water that the beans have been cooked in). I don't recommend cooking dry beans from scratch in it—the stock's acidity may retard the softening process.

3 or 4   carrots, washed and chopped
2   bell peppers, diced
2   large onions, diced
4   celery stalks, diced
4 to 6   whole garlic cloves
1   bunch broccoli, diced
1   small bunch parsley, diced
About 6 cups water, to cover

Place all of the ingredients in a large stockpot and cover with the water. Simmer for 1 to 2 hours. Add more water to keep the vegetables immersed if necessary.

Strain the vegetables and save the liquid. Discard the vegetables and use the liquid for soups and sauces. If kept refrigerated, the stock should last for about 5 to 7 days.

Yield: about 4 cups

Each serving provides:

36		Calories	8	g	Carbohydrate
2	g	Protein	27	mg	Sodium
0	g	Fat	0	mg	Cholesterol
2	g	Dietary Fiber			

A Big Bowl of Red

Nothing chases the winter blues away better than a bowl of homemade chili—or a bowl of red, as some affectionately call it. Here is an updated meatless version perfect for a snowy afternoon or, come to think of it, anytime you are in the mood for something hearty. The liberal use of seasonings is one of my secrets in achieving a flavorful, exuberant chili.

2 tablespoons vegetable oil
1 large onion, diced
1 green bell pepper, seeded and diced
1 red bell pepper, seeded and diced
1 cup sliced celery
2 cloves garlic, minced
1 jalapeño pepper, seeded and minced
1 large tomato, cored and diced
1 can (28 ounces) crushed tomatoes
2 cups cooked or canned red kidney beans, drained
1 to 1½ tablespoons chili powder
1 tablespoon dried oregano
2 to 3 teaspoons ground cumin
1 teaspoon paprika
1 teaspoon salt
1 to 3 teaspoons Tabasco or other bottled hot sauce
½ teaspoon ground black pepper

Lean Bean Cuisine

Heat the oil in a large saucepan and add the onion, bell peppers, celery, garlic, and jalapeño. Sauté for 6 to 8 minutes, until the vegetables are tender. Add the fresh tomato and cook for 3 to 4 minutes more. Stir in the canned crushed tomatoes, kidney beans, and seasonings and simmer for about 30 minutes over low heat, stirring occasionally. Ladle the chili into bowls and serve hot.

Yield: 4 servings

Each serving provides:

278	Calories	43 g	Carbohydrate
12 g	Protein	951 mg	Sodium
9 g	Fat	0 mg	Cholesterol
8 g	Dietary Fiber		

Variation:
Sprinkle shredded provolone cheese, diced red onion, scallions, or cilantro over the top. Or spoon a dollop of light sour cream onto the chili.

Beans, Greens, and Salads

This chapter offers a carnival of flavors, textures, and colors. Beans make a versatile salad ingredient, whether as a solo performer or as a member of an all-star ensemble of pasta, rice, green leafy vegetables, potatoes, or squash. Beans provide the spark for a medley of refreshing, crunchy salads.

Of course, history is not on the side of beans here. Bean salads have their own kind of culinary baggage. The three-bean salads of the past, with their tinny, monotone flavors and packed-in-formaldehyde appearance, are not at the top of anyone's short list of most beloved salads. But once you wipe out those blighted memories, bean salad enlightenment is only a tablespoon of cilantro or parsley away. A dash of hot sauce or sprig of mint is around the corner, and bean salads are on their way to a new image.

Many of the salads in this chapter make ideal picnic fare. Imagine a picnic basket filled with Lentil, Apple, and Bow Tie Pasta Salad or Sicilian Ceci Bean and Pasta Salad. Or Two-Bean Salad with Mint Tahini Sauce; Black Bean, Beet, and Jicama Salad; or Spa Bean Salad with Balsamic-Basil Vinaigrette. For an exotic salad at home, try Island Heat Salad with Spinach, Goat Cheese, and Red Beans. The possibilities beckon.

When preparing beans for salads, cook them until they are tender but still firm—almost like pasta al dente. For the sake of convenience, I have included quite a few recipes for canned beans.

As with most salads, it is best to allow the flavors to meld together for at least an hour before serving. If you combine the beans with the other salad ingredients while they are still warm, the flavors will sink in better. Fresh and dried herbs and light oil-and-vinegar dressings deliver subtle shades of flavors to many of the recipes.

Freshen up your bean salads at the last minute with finely chopped scallions, parsley, or other green herbs. And for an easy but decorative presentation, serve the bean salads over a bed of leafy greens such as romaine lettuce or green-leaf lettuce and garnish with shredded carrots, jicama, or red cabbage.

White Bean
and Sweet Potato Salad

Here is a quick and easy picnic salad. White beans step into the leading role in this salad with much aplomb. Sweet potatoes, rich in beta carotene, have always been a favorite salad ingredient of mine. The inclusion of leafy green vegetables rounds out the dish, and sneaks in even more nutrients (and flavor). Scrub the potatoes, but don't peel them.

4   cups diced sweet potatoes (2 large potatoes)
1½   cups cooked or canned navy
         or great northern beans, drained
1   cup shredded mustard greens
         or dandelion greens
½   cup slivered red onion
½   cup chopped celery
2   tablespoons minced fresh parsley
½ to ¾   cup vegetable oil
⅓   cup red wine vinegar
1   teaspoon sugar
1   teaspoon dried thyme
¼   teaspoon ground black pepper
¼   teaspoon salt

Place the sweet potatoes in boiling water to cover and cook for about 15 minutes, until they are easily pierced with a fork. Drain and chill under cold running water.

Combine the potatoes with the remaining ingredients in a mixing bowl and blend thoroughly. Chill for at least 1 hour before serving.

Yield: 6 to 8 servings

Each serving provides:

322	Calories	32 g	Carbohydrate
5 g	Protein	99 mg	Sodium
20 g	Fat	0 mg	Cholesterol
4 g	Dietary Fiber		

Mediterranean Couscous and Lentil Salad

Lentils have been appearing in salads on more and more restaurant menus lately, and that's good news for health-conscious customers. Here they are combined with easy-to-prepare couscous and Mediterranean flavors for a light, vibrant salad. Although it is not mandatory, soaking the lentils for an hour will expedite the cooking time.

½ cup brown or red lentils
3 cups water
1 cup boiling water
⅔ cup uncooked couscous
¼ cup vegetable oil
2 tablespoons red wine vinegar
1 teaspoon Dijon-style mustard
2 tablespoons chopped fresh basil
1 tablespoon minced fresh parsley
1 teaspoon dried oregano
½ teaspoon salt
¼ teaspoon ground black pepper
1 red bell pepper, seeded and diced
3 or 4 scallions, chopped
2 cloves garlic, minced

Place the lentils and water in a saucepan and cook for 45 minutes, until tender. Drain the lentils in a colander.

Meanwhile, combine the couscous and boiling water in a small saucepan, cover, and let stand for 10 minutes.

In a mixing bowl, whisk together the oil, vinegar, mustard, herbs, and seasonings. Add the lentils, bell pepper, scallions, garlic, and couscous and blend well. Chill for 1 hour before serving.

Yield: 4 servings

Each serving provides:

335	Calories	41 g	Carbohydrate
11 g	Protein	320 mg	Sodium
14 g	Fat	0 mg	Cholesterol
5 g	Dietary Fiber		

Warm Quinoa, Corn, and Cranberry Bean Salad

Quinoa (say "keen-wa") is a grain indigenous to South America and can be traced all the way back to the Inca civilization. Lately it has been hailed as a "super grain" because of its high protein content. It is similar to rice in texture and is a natural partner for cranberry beans, another native food. Pink beans may be substituted.

1 cup quinoa, rinsed
2 cups water
2 cups cooked or canned cranberry beans
  or pink beans, drained
4 scallions, finely chopped
1 red bell pepper, seeded and diced
1 cup corn kernels, fresh, frozen, or canned
1 tablespoon minced fresh cilantro
1 teaspoon dried oregano
½ teaspoon ground cumin
¼ teaspoon ground black pepper
¼ teaspoon salt

Lean Bean Cuisine

Place the quinoa and water in a saucepan and bring to a simmer. Cover and cook for about 15 minutes over medium heat, until all of the water is absorbed. Set aside.

In a mixing bowl, combine the beans, scallions, bell pepper, corn, cilantro, and seasonings and blend well. Blend in the quinoa. Serve warm, or chill and serve at a later time as a cold salad with vinaigrette dressing.

Yield: 4 servings

Each serving provides:

325	Calories	61 g	Carbohydrate
16 g	Protein	171 mg	Sodium
3 g	Fat	0 mg	Cholesterol
11 g	Dietary Fiber		

Black Bean, Beet, and Jicama Salad

Beets, like beans, carry a lot of baggage with them. Lunch at the high school cafeteria comes to mind: images of canned beets sitting on the side of the plate looking bored, spilling runny red juice all over the place. But fresh beets have come a long way, especially when combined with black beans and jicama to form a tasty, colorful salad. The jicama provides the crispy crunch, and horseradish adds a pleasant zip.

3 or 4   beets, peeled and diced
2   tablespoons vegetable oil
2   tablespoons rice vinegar or other vinegar
1½ teaspoons prepared horseradish
1   teaspoon Dijon-style mustard
1   tablespoon minced fresh parsley
¼   teaspoon ground black pepper
¼   teaspoon salt
1½ cups cooked or canned black beans, drained
1   cup peeled, diced jicama (or carrot)
4   leaves of lettuce
1   teaspoon sesame seeds

Place the beets in boiling water to cover, and cook for 20 to 25 minutes, until tender. Drain and cool under cold running water.

In a mixing bowl, whisk together the oil, vinegar, horseradish, mustard, and seasonings. Add the beets, beans, and jicama and blend well. Chill at least 1 hour before serving. Serve the salad on a bed of leaf lettuce and sprinkle sesame seeds over the top.

Yield: 4 servings

Each serving provides:

199	Calories	26 g	Carbohydrate
7 g	Protein	231 mg	Sodium
8 g	Fat	0 mg	Cholesterol
3 g	Dietary Fiber		

Lima Bean
and Kohlrabi Salad
with Szechuan Peanut Sauce

*Kohlrabi is a pale green, bulbous vegetable with a smooth,
crunchy texture and a mild celery and broccoli-like flavor. The
lima beans are also low-key. Then along comes the Szechuan
peanut sauce, and boom! It's a welcome invasion of strong
Asian flavors. The result is a low baritone-flavored salad
balanced with a high-pitched brass section of Szechuan peanut
sauce.*

2   cloves garlic, chopped
1   tablespoon chopped fresh ginger root
1   cup unsalted peanut butter
⅓   cup light soy sauce
2   tablespoons bottled Szechuan hot sauce
2   tablespoons lime juice
1   tablespoon dark sesame oil
2   cups cooked or canned small lima beans, drained
8   cauliflower florets, blanched
2   small kohlrabi bulbs, peeled and diced
4   scallions, chopped
1   red bell pepper, seeded and diced

To make the sauce, add the garlic and ginger to a food processor fitted with a steel blade and process 10 seconds, until finely chopped. Add the peanut butter, soy sauce, Szechuan sauce, lime juice, and sesame oil and process for 10 to 15 seconds more. Transfer the sauce to a mixing bowl, add the beans, cauliflower, kohlrabi, scallions, and bell pepper and blend well. Chill for 1 hour before serving.

Serve the salad on a bed of lettuce.

Yield: 6 to 8 servings

Each serving provides:

338	Calories	25 g	Carbohydrate
15 g	Protein	586 mg	Sodium
22 g	Fat	0 mg	Cholesterol
6 g	Dietary Fiber		

Sicilian Ceci Bean and Pasta Salad

Ceci (pronounced "chee-chee") beans is the Italian name for chick peas. Their nutty flavor and firm texture make them a favorite salad ingredient. This is a good salad to take along to the ball park or outdoor jazz concert.

4   cups uncooked pasta spirals
½ cup red wine vinegar
¾ cup olive oil or other vegetable oil
1   tablespoon Dijon-style mustard
2   tablespoons minced fresh parsley
1   tablespoon dried oregano
1   tablespoon dried basil
1   teaspoon dried thyme
½ teaspoon ground black pepper
¼ teaspoon salt
2   cups cooked or canned ceci beans
     (chick peas), drained
6 to 8   pepperoncini, chopped
4   plum tomatoes, diced
4 to 6   scallions, diced
⅓ pound mozzarella cheese, cubed

Place the pasta in boiling water and cook for 9 to 11 minutes, until al dente. Drain in a colander and cool under cold running water.

In a large mixing bowl, whisk together the vinegar, oil, mustard, and seasonings. Add the cooked pasta, ceci beans, pepperonci, tomatoes, scallions, and cheese, and blend well. Chill for 1 hour before serving.

Serve the salad on a bed of lettuce.

Yield: 6 to 8 servings

Each serving provides:

473		Calories	40 g	Carbohydrate
13	g	Protein	231 mg	Sodium
30	g	Fat	17 mg	Cholesterol
4	g	Dietary Fiber		

Three-Bean Salad with Greek Flavors

The traditional three-bean salad has long been in need of a makeover. Here the beans are tossed with a light vinaigrette and accented with Greek herbal flavors and feta cheese. This will help you forget those pale, anemic-looking three-bean salads loitering at the salad bar.

1   cup cooked or canned navy beans
      or other small white beans, drained
1   cup cooked or canned chick peas
1   cup cooked or canned red kidney beans
½   cup coarsely chopped fresh mint leaves
1   unpeeled cucumber, diced
2 or 3   scallions, chopped
2   plum tomatoes, chopped
¼   pound feta cheese, crumbled
2   cloves garlic, minced
2   tablespoons rice or wine vinegar
2   tablespoons olive oil
2   tablespoons minced fresh parsley
      (or 1 tablespoon dried)
1   teaspoon dried thyme
½   teaspoon ground black pepper
¼   teaspoon salt

Combine all of the ingredients in a mixing bowl and blend thoroughly. Chill for 1 hour before serving.

Serve on a bed of leaf lettuce.

Yield: 4 servings

Each serving provides:

344	Calories	39 g	Carbohydrate
16 g	Protein	463 mg	Sodium
15 g	Fat	25 mg	Cholesterol
6 g	Dietary Fiber		

Tabooley with Chick Peas
(Wheat Garden Salad)

Tabooley, or tabbouleh, is a Middle Eastern salad of cracked wheat (bulgur), lemon, parsley, and tomatoes. There are a host of variable ingredients, such as chick peas, black-eyed peas, and assorted garden vegetables. This is my grandmother's version, as best as I could transcribe it. She has made tabooley for a long, long time, since way before it became trendy.

1   cup fine cracked wheat (bulgur)
2   cups boiling water
2   scallions, chopped
½   cup chopped fresh parsley
2   tablespoons minced fresh mint
      (or 1 tablespoon dried)
4   plum tomatoes, diced
1   cucumber, peeled and diced
1   cup cooked or canned chick peas, drained
Juice of 1 to 2 lemons
¼   cup olive oil
½   teaspoon ground black pepper
½   teaspoon salt

Combine the wheat and boiling water in a small saucepan, cover, and let sit for 30 minutes to 1 hour, until all of the water is absorbed.

In a mixing bowl, combine the cracked wheat with the remaining ingredients. Chill until ready to serve. Serve with green, leafy lettuce on the side and pita bread.

Yield: 4 servings

Each serving provides:

331	Calories	44 g	Carbohydrate
9 g	Protein	293 mg	Sodium
15 g	Fat	0 mg	Cholesterol
9 g	Dietary Fiber		

Black-Eyed Pea Salad with Pasta Wheels and Asparagus

In this salad, high-society asparagus meets the humble legume. The enticing, salad-friendly pasta wheels are an accommodating medium, and the result is a splendid dish. Chick peas and red kidney beans also work well in this salad.

2   cups uncooked pasta wheels
12   stalks asparagus, sliced ¾ to 1 inch thick
¼   cup olive oil or vegetable oil
2   tablespoons red wine vinegar
2   tablespoons minced fresh parsley
½   teaspoon ground black pepper
½   teaspoon salt
2   cups cooked or canned black-eyed peas,
      chick peas, or kidney beans, drained
2 or 3   scallions, chopped
2   tomatoes, cored and diced
1   cup corn kernels, fresh, frozen, or canned
¼   cup grated Parmesan cheese

Place the pasta in boiling water and cook for 8 to 10 minutes, until al dente. Drain in a colander and cool under cold running water.

Meanwhile, place the asparagus in boiling water to cover and boil for 3 minutes. Drain and discard the water.

In a large mixing bowl, whisk together the oil, vinegar, and seasonings. Add the pasta, asparagus, and remaining ingredients and blend well. Chill for 1 hour before serving.

Serve the salad on a bed of lettuce.

Yield: 4 to 6 servings

Each serving provides:

397	Calories	56 g	Carbohydrate
15 g	Protein	310 mg	Sodium
14 g	Fat	3 mg	Cholesterol
10 g	Dietary Fiber		

Two-Bean Salad with Mint Tahini Sauce

Tahini is a sesame paste with the consistency of natural peanut butter. The paste adds a nutty flavor to beans, and is complemented by the springtime scent of mint.

2   cups small Green Fordhook lima beans,
        frozen or canned, drained
2   cups cooked or canned butter beans
        or large white beans, drained
½   cup tahini (sesame paste)
1   cucumber, diced
1   cup plain nonfat yogurt
2   tablespoons lemon juice
2   cloves garlic, minced
2   tablespoons coarsely chopped fresh mint leaves
        (or 1 tablespoon dried)
2   tablespoons minced fresh parsley
1   teaspoon paprika
½   teaspoon salt
¼   teaspoon cayenne pepper

To cook the lima beans, place in boiling water to cover and cook for about 10 minutes, until soft. Drain in a colander and cool under cold running water.

Blend together the remaining ingredients in a serving bowl. Stir in the lima beans and chill for 30 minutes before serving. Serve on a bed of leaf lettuce.

Yield: 4 servings

Each serving provides:

457	Calories	57 g	Carbohydrate
24 g	Protein	403 mg	Sodium
17 g	Fat	1 mg	Cholesterol
7 g	Dietary Fiber		

Spa Bean Salad with Balsamic-Basil Vinaigrette

"Spa" does not always have to mean bland, sterile food. I picture spa food as healthful and lively with sprightly flavors. For a smoky variation, roast the red bell pepper over a fire and remove the skin before dicing it.

2 cups cooked or canned black-eyed peas, drained
2 cups cooked or canned small lima beans
   or chick peas, drained
1 cup cooked red or brown lentils
4 scallions, chopped
1 red bell pepper, seeded and diced
1 tablespoon minced shallots
3 tablespoons olive or vegetable oil
2 tablespoons balsamic vinegar
2 tablespoons chopped fresh basil
   (or 2 teaspoons dried)
¾ teaspoon ground black pepper
½ teaspoon salt

Combine all of the ingredients in a large mixing bowl and blend well. Chill for 1 hour before serving. Serve on a bed of leaf lettuce.

Yield: 4 servings

Each serving provides:

356	Calories	49 g	Carbohydrate
18 g	Protein	307 mg	Sodium
11 g	Fat	0 mg	Cholesterol
14 g	Dietary Fiber		

Harvest Beet, Potato, and Large Bean Salad

Say good-bye to the gloppy, mayonnaise-laden potato salads of yesteryear. Beans, with the help of fresh beets and dill, form a perfect alliance with potatoes and add bold color, texture, and most of all, refreshing flavor.

If you are still peeling potatoes before you use them, stop it. The potato's skin is filled with valuable nutrients and flavor. A good scrubbing will do.

2	cups diced fresh beets
4	cups diced new potatoes or Yukon Gold potatoes
¼	cup rice vinegar
¼	cup vegetable oil
1	tablespoon Dijon-style mustard
¼	cup chopped fresh dill
½	teaspoon ground black pepper
½	teaspoon salt
1½	cups cooked or canned white cannellini beans or large lima beans, drained
1	cup diced celery
1	bunch scallions, chopped

Place the beets in boiling water to cover and cook for 20 to 25 minutes, until the beets are easily pierced with a fork, but still firm. Drain and cool under cold running water.

In another saucepan, place the potatoes in boiling water to cover and cook for about 15 minutes, until easily pierced with a fork. Drain and cool under cold running water.

In a mixing bowl, whisk together the vinegar, oil, mustard, and seasonings. Add the beans, potatoes, beets, celery, and scallions, and blend well. Chill at least 1 hour before serving.

Serve the salad on a bed of leaf lettuce.

Yield: 6 to 8 servings

Each serving provides:

213	Calories	31 g	Carbohydrate
5 g	Protein	281 mg	Sodium
8 g	Fat	0 mg	Cholesterol
4 g	Dietary Fiber		

Southwestern Lentil and Couscous Salad

The bright flavors and colors of the Southwest inspired this delightful creation.

1	cup brown or red lentils
4	cups water
⅔	cup uncooked couscous
1	cup boiling water
1	cup corn kernels, fresh, frozen, or canned
1	red bell pepper, seeded and diced
3 or 4	scallions, chopped
1	jalapeño pepper, seeded and minced (optional)
2	tablespoons vegetable oil
2	tablespoons minced fresh cilantro
1	tablespoon red wine vinegar
2 to 3	teaspoons Tabasco or other bottled hot sauce
1	teaspoon ground cumin
½	teaspoon salt
½	teaspoon ground black pepper

Place the lentils and water in a saucepan and simmer over medium heat for 40 to 45 minutes, until tender. Drain and chill.

Combine the couscous and boiling water in a bowl, cover, and let stand for 10 minutes.

In a mixing bowl, combine the lentils, couscous, and all of the remaining ingredients and blend well. Chill for 1 hour before serving.

Yield: 4 servings

Each serving provides:

384		Calories	61	g	Carbohydrate
19	g	Protein	312	mg	Sodium
8	g	Fat	0	mg	Cholesterol
9	g	Dietary Fiber			

Lentil, Apple, and Bow Tie Pasta Salad

My friend Beth Ryan is a marathon runner who likes to carbo-load before a big race. We created a healthful pasta salad that not only meets Beth's substantial carbohydrate needs, but also satisfies the palate of any discerning gourmand as well. Apples provide a crispy crunch to the salad. Whether you're a runner or not, you will enjoy this delectable combination.

½   cup dried lentils (any kind)
3   cups water
8   ounces bow tie pasta *(farfalle)*
8 to 10   cherry tomatoes, halved
4   scallions, chopped
2   apples, cored and diced
1   yellow or green bell pepper, seeded and diced
½   cup olive oil
¼   cup balsamic vinegar or red wine vinegar
¼   cup fresh basil leaves, chopped
     (or 1 tablespoon dried)
2   cloves garlic, minced
2   tablespoons minced fresh parsley
     (or 1 tablespoon dried)
½   teaspoon salt
¼   teaspoon dried red pepper flakes
¼   cup grated Parmesan cheese

Place the lentils and water in a saucepan and simmer over medium heat for 40 to 45 minutes, until tender. Drain the lentils and chill.

Meanwhile, place the bow ties in boiling water to cover and cook for about 12 minutes, until al dente. Drain in a colander and cool under cold running water.

In a large bowl, combine the lentils, pasta, and remaining ingredients and blend well. Chill for 30 minutes to 1 hour before serving.

Serve on a bed of leaf lettuce.

Yield: 6 servings

Each serving provides:

411	Calories	48 g	Carbohydrate
11 g	Protein	253 mg	Sodium
20 g	Fat	3 mg	Cholesterol
4 g	Dietary Fiber		

Island Heat Salad
with Spinach, Goat Cheese,
and Red Beans

While vacationing on St. John's, one of the Virgin Islands,
I was treated to a dinner salad that was actually cooked, not
the usual cold combination of raw vegetables and greens. It
was a pleasant detour from the standard fare. This version is
an adaptation of that island salad, using spinach and red beans.

3   tablespoons vegetable oil
2   tablespoons red wine vinegar
1   medium carrot, peeled and shredded
½   cup shredded jicama
½   cup shredded red cabbage
4 to 6   cherry tomatoes, halved
2   scallions, chopped
1   whole Scotch bonnet, jalapeño,
        or other hot chile pepper, punctured with a fork
1   cup packed fresh spinach leaves, chopped
1   cup chopped green or red leaf lettuce
1   cup cooked or canned small red chili beans
        or pigeon peas, drained
2   ounces smooth goat cheese, chopped
Salt and pepper, to taste

Heat the oil and vinegar in a skillet. Add the carrot, jicama, cabbage, tomatoes, scallions, and chile pepper and sauté for about 5 minutes. Add the spinach, lettuce, and beans and cook for about 3 minutes more, stirring frequently. Blend in the goat cheese and seasonings and cook for 1 minute more.

Remove the vegetables from the heat and serve hot on a plate. Take out the chile pepper and give it to the hot foods aficionado at the table.

Yield: 2 servings

Each serving provides:

419		Calories	33	g	Carbohydrate
14	g	Protein	165	mg	Sodium
27	g	Fat	13	mg	Cholesterol
8	g	Dietary Fiber			

Pasta and Red Bean Salad with Pesto

Pesto is a potent taste of garlic, basil, nuts, and cheese. The ingredients are traditionally crushed together using a mortar and pestle (hence the name "pesto"). Nowadays, a food processor does the trick. The melange of enticing flavors is a welcome guest in this salad of pasta and beans. One caveat: dried basil cannot be substituted for fresh basil in this recipe.

For the pesto:
4 to 6   cloves garlic, coarsely chopped
¼   cup cashews or pine nuts
1½   cups packed fresh basil leaves
½   cup olive oil
1   teaspoon ground black pepper
1   teaspoon salt
½   cup grated Parmesan cheese or Romano cheese

For the salad:
½   pound uncooked pasta shells or spirals
10 to 12   yellow or red cherry tomatoes, halved
4   scallions, chopped
½   cup shredded carrots
2   cups cooked or canned red kidney beans
    or chick peas, drained

To make the pesto, add the garlic and nuts to a food processor fitted with a steel blade. Process for 15 seconds. Add the basil, oil, and seasonings and process for 15 seconds more, until smooth. Transfer to a bowl and blend in the cheese.

Place the pasta in boiling water to cover, and cook for 9 to 12 minutes, until al dente. Drain in a colander and cool under cold running water.

In a large mixing bowl, combine the pesto with the pasta, vegetables, and beans and blend well. Chill for 1 hour.

Serve on a bed of lettuce.

Yield: 4 to 6 servings

Each serving provides:

553	Calories	59 g	Carbohydrate
18 g	Protein	604 mg	Sodium
29 g	Fat	6 mg	Cholesterol
5 g	Dietary Fiber		

Bolivian Bean Salad

I've adapted this recipe from my friend Jessica, who was a Peace Corps volunteer in Bolivia. It is traditionally made with haba beans, a large Bolivian bean similar to fava beans. I have substituted Jacob's cattle beans, a mottled bean named for the cattlelike design on its skin. Red kidney beans or large fava beans will also work.

2   cups cooked Jacob's cattle beans,
        kidney beans, or fava beans, drained
2   tomatoes, cored and diced
⅓   pound crumbled feta cheese
1   red onion, diced
1   small Scotch bonnet
        or other hot chile pepper, seeded and minced
2 to 3   tablespoons vegetable oil
¼   teaspoon salt

Combine all of the ingredients in a large mixing bowl and blend well. Chill for at least 1 hour before serving. Serve with a tossed salad.

Yield: 4 servings

Each serving provides:

317	Calories	29 g	Carbohydrate
14 g	Protein	565 mg	Sodium
17 g	Fat	33 mg	Cholesterol
5 g	Dietary Fiber		

Appealing Appetizers and Dipping Sauces

Appetizers and small dishes are all the rage in some culinary circles. The more little dishes there are at the table, the greater the eating experience. And appetizers are often served at a time when you are the most hungry—all the more reason to make them a memorable part of your meal.

Too often, however, appetizer fare is a platter of greasy, fried clumps masquerading as finger food. As a prelude to the meal to come, appetizers and dipping sauces should excite your appetite, not depress it. The ambition of this chapter is to offer adventurous first courses that stimulate your palate without clotting your arteries at the same time. If a meal were a concert, the ideal appetizer would be an upbeat piano solo that gently catches your ear.

Beans, therefore, are a welcome addition to the staid world of grazing food. Many of the dishes in this chapter feature small bites with big flavors. Quesadillas with Black Beans, Corn, and Avocado; Crostini with Tuscan-Style Beans and Braised Greens; Piquant Black Bean and Red Tomato Salsa; Pureed Yellow Split Peas (Channa Dal); and Middle Eastern Hummus with Herbal Flavors are some of the tantalizing first courses. The recipes can also be served as a side dish or as a light meal with tossed salad, rice, or pasta.

By the way, potential appetizers are not limited to this chapter. Explore the book, and if a dish strikes your fancy, try serving it in smaller portions. These days, just about anything goes if it tastes good.

Quesadillas
with Black Beans, Corn,
and Avocado

Here is a great way to start a meal. Homemade quesadillas are quick and easy to make, and a vast improvement over most restaurant offerings. The colorful combination of beans, corn, avocadoes, and tomatoes is as pleasing to the eye as it is to the palate.

2	ripe avocadoes, peeled, pitted, and cut into ¾-inch chunks
2	tomatoes, cored and diced
6	scallions, chopped
1	cup cooked or canned black beans or pinto beans, drained
1	cup corn kernels, fresh, frozen, or canned
1	cup shredded Monterey jack or provolone cheese
1 or 2	jalapeño peppers, seeded and minced
½	teaspoon ground cumin
2	tablespoons minced fresh cilantro
8	(6-inch) flour tortillas

Preheat the oven to 400°F.

Place 4 tortillas on a lightly greased baking pan. Layer an equal amount of avocado, tomato, scallions, beans, corn, cheese, and jalapeño on each of the tortillas, forming small mounds. Season with cumin and cilantro. Lay the remaining tortillas over the tops and place in the oven. Bake for 10 to 12 minutes, or until the tortillas are lightly browned.

Transfer the quesadillas to round serving plates. Cut into wedges and serve with your favorite salsa and/or guacamole.

Yield: 4 to 6 appetizers

Each serving provides:

417		Calories	42	g	Carbohydrate
15	g	Protein	296	mg	Sodium
23	g	Fat	24	mg	Cholesterol
5	g	Dietary Fiber			

Crostini
with Tuscan-Style Beans
and Braised Greens

In Tuscany, white cannellini beans and cranberry beans are the favored legumes. They are traditionally seasoned with sage, garlic, and olive oil and added to soups and salads such as Tuscan Bean Soup with Leafy Green Vegetables (page 28). Here they are served as an enlightened appetizer with braised greens. Crostini *means "little crusts" in Italian and evolved as a way to use up yesterday's bread.*

½	cup cranberry or cannellini beans, soaked and drained
2½	cups water
1	small onion, diced
1	teaspoon dried sage
½	teaspoon dried thyme
2	tablespoons olive oil
2	cloves garlic, minced
1	red or green bell pepper, seeded and diced
¼	teaspoon dried red pepper flakes
2	cups chopped, packed spinach or Swiss chard
2	tablespoons water
½	teaspoon salt
6 to 8	thick slices Italian bread, toasted

Place the beans, water, onion, sage, and thyme in a saucepan and cook for 1 hour, until tender. Drain any excess liquid and keep warm.

In a saucepan, heat the oil over medium heat and add the garlic, bell pepper, and red pepper flakes. Cook for 3 to 4 minutes. Add the greens, water, and salt and cook for 3 to 4 minutes more, stirring occasionally. Add the beans and cook for 2 to 3 minutes more.

Spread the beans-and-greens mixture over the toasted bread. Serve at once.

Yield: 6 servings

Each serving provides:

195	Calories	29	g	Carbohydrate
8 g	Protein	382	mg	Sodium
6 g	Fat	0	mg	Cholesterol
4 g	Dietary Fiber			

Middle Eastern Hummus with Herbal Flavors

If you've been to a natural foods deli in the past decade, you will recognize this dish. Hummus is a popular and versatile puree of chick peas, tahini, and lemon juice. I've improvised by adding a hint of fresh herbs. It makes a tasty sandwich filling, salad dressing, or vegetable dip.

2   cups cooked or canned chick peas, drained
¼   cup lemon juice
¼   cup tahini (sesame paste)
¼   cup water
2   cloves garlic, minced
1 to 2   tablespoons fresh minced chives, savory, or marjoram
¼   teaspoon ground white pepper
¼   teaspoon salt

Combine all of the ingredients in a food processor fitted with a steel blade and process for 15 seconds, until the mixture is the consistency of a thick pancake batter. Transfer to a serving bowl and serve with raw vegetables, over a salad, or in a sandwich. If refrigerated, hummus will keep for 5 to 7 days.

Yield: 2½ cups

Each serving provides:

23	Calories	3 g	Carbohydrate
1 g	Protein	16 mg	Sodium
1 g	Fat	0 mg	Cholesterol
0 g	Dietary Fiber		

Pureed Yellow Split Peas (Channa Dal)

Dal is an Indian dish of pureed legumes. Indians use an assortment of lentils, split peas, mung beans, and chick peas for dal. (Channa dal is made from yellow split peas.) The legumes are cooked until they reach a melt-in-your-mouth consistency. A combination of spicy curry seasonings gives the split peas a rich, earthy flavor. Dal is traditionally served with sautéed onions and bread or rice. It also makes a good roti filling (page 150).

1   cup yellow split peas or any type of lentil, rinsed
4   cups water
¼   teaspoon ground turmeric
2   tablespoons vegetable oil
1   small onion, diced
1   tomato, cored and chopped
2   cloves garlic, minced
½   tablespoon minced fresh ginger root
1   jalapeño or serrano pepper, seeded and minced
½   teaspoon garam masala
¼   teaspoon ground cumin
¼   teaspoon ground coriander
¼   teaspoon salt
1   tablespoon chopped fresh cilantro

In a saucepan, combine the split peas, water, and turmeric and simmer for 45 minutes to 1 hour over medium heat, until the peas are tender.

Heat the oil in a skillet and add the onion. Cook for about 5 minutes over medium heat. Stir in the tomato, garlic, ginger, and jalapeño and cook for 5 to 7 minutes more. Add the seasonings to the pan and cook for 1 minute more, stirring frequently.

At this point, you may either spoon the cooked split peas into a bowl and top with the onion-curry mixture, or combine the split peas and curry-onion mixture in the skillet. Keep warm until ready to serve.

Yield: 4 servings

Each serving provides:

251	Calories	35 g	Carbohydrate
13 g	Protein	147 mg	Sodium
8 g	Fat	0 mg	Cholesterol
4 g	Dietary Fiber		

Large Lima Beans
with Greek Skordalia Sauce

Skordalia is a garlicky (and some would say heavenly) sauce with roots in Greek cuisine. The sauce is a thin potato puree, sort of a slimmed down, velvety version of mashed potatoes. Traditionally, skordalia is served with large lima beans (also called gigandes) *and wild greens or beet greens. Garnish with fresh mint or basil.*

This is one of the few recipes for which I recommend peeling the potatoes first.

2   cups peeled, diced white potatoes
6 to 8   cloves garlic, chopped
½   cup olive oil
¼   cup red wine vinegar
1   tablespoon lemon juice
¼   teaspoon salt
¼   teaspoon ground white pepper
4   cups cooked or canned large lima beans
        or butter beans, drained and warmed

Place the potatoes in boiling water to cover and cook for about 20 minutes, until easily pierced with a fork. Drain and cool slightly.

Add the garlic to a food processor fitted with a steel blade and process for about 10 seconds, until minced. Add the potatoes and process for 15 to 20 seconds more, until smooth. With the motor running, drizzle in the oil, vinegar, lemon juice, and seasonings and process until the sauce is the consistency of mayonnaise. Scrape the skordalia into a serving bowl.

Place the beans on serving plates and spoon the skordalia sauce on the side. Garnish with fresh herbs. Savor every biteful.

Yield: 6 servings

Each serving provides:

345	Calories	38 g	Carbohydrate
9 g	Protein	113 mg	Sodium
18 g	Fat	0 mg	Cholesterol
6 g	Dietary Fiber		

Piquant Black Bean and Red Tomato Salsa

This salsa always garners rave reviews at my cooking classes. The primary flavors—cilantro, chiles, and lime juice—envelop the beans with an inviting taste. There are many versions of salsa; this combines the tang of a tomato salsa with the heartiness of a salad. To make it hotter, add more chiles or liberally douse it with your favorite bottled hot sauce.

2	tomatoes, cored and diced
1	green bell pepper, seeded and diced
1	medium onion, diced
2 or 3	cloves garlic, minced
1 or 2	serrano or jalapeño peppers, seeded and minced
1	tablespoon minced fresh cilantro
2	teaspoons lime juice
1½	teaspoons ground cumin
1	teaspoon dried oregano
¼	teaspoon black pepper
¼	teaspoon salt
⅛	teaspoon cayenne pepper
2	cups canned crushed tomatoes
1	cup cooked or canned black beans, drained

Combine all of the ingredients, except the crushed tomatoes and black beans, in a large bowl and blend well. Place three-quarters of the mixture in a food processor fitted with a steel blade and process for 5 seconds, creating a vegetable mash.

Return the mash to the bowl, add the crushed tomatoes and beans, and blend again. Cover the bowl tightly and chill for at least 1 hour, allowing the flavors to meld together.

Serve with Garden Vegetable and Black Bean Burrito (page 132), Breakfast Bean Burrito with Havarti Cheese (page 226), or tortilla chips.

Yield: 4 cups

Each serving provides:

31	Calories	6 g	Carbohydrate
2 g	Protein	85 mg	Sodium
0 g	Fat	0 mg	Cholesterol
1 g	Dietary Fiber		

Painless Black-Eyed Peas for New Year's Day

It is a New Year's Day ritual in some parts of the world to eat black-eyed peas for good luck. I guess that's why my mother shoved black-eyed peas down my throat like medicine every year during my childhood. She meant well, although she never fully explained what was going on.

Years later, my mother and I discussed this annual ritual/trauma, and we both decided it was time to update the annual rites with a more exciting dish. Here is what we came up with.

2   tablespoons vegetable oil
1   small green bell pepper, seeded and diced
2   cloves garlic, minced
1   tablespoon minced shallots
2   cups canned or cooked black-eyed peas, drained
1   tablespoon minced fresh parsley
1   teaspoon dried thyme
½   teaspoon ground black pepper
½   teaspoon salt
Tabasco or other bottled hot sauce, to taste

Heat the oil in a saucepan and add the bell pepper, garlic, and shallots. Sauté for 7 minutes. Add the peas, seasonings, and lots of hot sauce and cook for 10 minutes more over medium heat, stirring occasionally. Transfer to a serving bowl. Serve on New Year's Day for good luck.

Yield: 4 servings

Each serving provides:

166	Calories	19 g	Carbohydrate
6 g	Protein	456 mg	Sodium
7 g	Fat	0 mg	Cholesterol
5 g	Dietary Fiber		

Oozing Cheese and Bean Empanadas

Empanadas are savory turnovers popular in Latin American countries. There are many kinds of empanadas, but my favorite is this version, which oozes with cheese and beans. Traditional empanadas have a buttery, biscuitlike crust.

For a quick version, substitute 2 pounds of commercial biscuit dough for the homemade dough. Most supermarkets carry it in the refrigerated dairy section.

For the dough:
2½ cups all-purpose flour
1   tablespoon sugar
1   teaspoon baking powder
¾   teaspoon salt
¾   teaspoon ground nutmeg
¼   cup cold butter, chopped
¼   cup vegetable oil
3   egg yolks
1   cup milk

For the filling:
⅓   pound shredded Colby or Monterey jack cheese
2   cups cooked or canned red kidney beans
      or fava beans, drained
½   teaspoon paprika
½   teaspoon salt
¼   teaspoon cayenne pepper
2   egg whites

To make the dough, combine the flour, sugar, baking powder, salt, and nutmeg in a bowl. Blend in the butter with a pastry blender or fork until the mixture resembles coarse meal. Whisk in the oil, egg yolks, and half of the milk; gradually blend in the rest of the milk, forming a dough. Knead the dough briefly, until smooth, then set aside for 10 to 15 minutes.

To make the filling, combine the cheese, beans, paprika, salt, and pepper in a mixing bowl and blend well. Beat the egg whites in a separate bowl until they form stiff peaks, and then blend into the cheese and bean mixture.

Preheat the oven to 375°F.

Divide the dough into 6 equal balls. On a lightly floured board, roll each ball into a circle about ¼ inch thick. If the dough is too moist, sprinkle with a little flour. Place some of the bean and cheese mixture on one-half of each circle and then fold the dough over, enclosing the mixture and forming a half-moon shape. Press the edges with a fork to seal them and prick the surface several times.

Place the empanadas on a lightly greased baking sheet and bake for about 25 minutes, until golden brown. (If using commercial biscuit dough, follow the instructions on the package—most take only 10 minutes to bake.)

Remove from the oven and cool before serving.

Yield: 6 empanadas

Each serving provides:

593	Calories	60 g	Carbohydrate
21 g	Protein	811 mg	Sodium
30 g	Fat	156 mg	Cholesterol
4 g	Dietary Fiber		

Jamaican Patties with Callaloo and Pigeon Peas

Jamaican patties are Caribbean turnovers distantly related to empanadas. Although traditionally filled with meat, vegetables such as callaloo (a spinachlike leafy green) are gradually becoming the preferred filling. Callaloo is hard to find, but you can substitute collard greens or spinach. These patties are served as appetizers or as a light lunch, often accompanied by mixed greens and rice.

As with empanadas, substitute 2 pounds of commercial biscuit dough if you don't have time to make the pastry.

For the pastry:
4   cups all-purpose flour
1   teaspoon baking powder
1   teaspoon salt
1   cup margarine or shortening
½   cup water

For the filling:
1   tablespoon butter or vegetable oil
1   medium onion, finely chopped
1   red bell pepper, seeded and finely chopped
1   jalapeño pepper, seeded and minced
1   cup precooked callaloo or spinach, chopped
1   cup cooked or canned pigeon peas
      or small red chili beans, drained
½   teaspoon dried thyme
½   teaspoon ground black pepper
¼   teaspoon salt

1   tablespoon annatto oil or vegetable oil

To make the pastry, combine the flour, baking powder, and salt in a mixing bowl. With a pastry blender or a fork, cut in the margarine until the mixture resembles coarse meal. Mix in the water and form a ball. Chill for 15 minutes. Preheat the oven to 375°F.

In a skillet, heat the butter and sauté the onion, bell pepper, and jalapeño for 5 to 7 minutes, until the vegetables are soft. Add the callaloo, beans, and seasonings and cook for 5 minutes more. Remove from the heat and cool.

Divide the dough into 8 equal-sized balls. With a rolling pin, roll each ball into a circle about ¼ inch thick. Spoon some of the callaloo mixture onto one-half of each circle and fold over the dough, enclosing the mixture and forming a half-moon shape. Press the edges with a fork to seal.

Place the patties on a lightly greased baking sheet and brush each patty with the annatto oil. Bake for 20 minutes, until the patties are golden brown. Serve warm with your favorite hot sauce.

Yield: 8 patties

Each serving provides:

502	Calories	57 g	Carbohydrate
9 g	Protein	705 mg	Sodium
27 g	Fat	4 mg	Cholesterol
4 g	Dietary Fiber		

Blazing Black Bean–
Scotch Bonnet Pepper Sauce

This black bean dip became an instant bestseller at my restaurant. The shining star is the fiery Scotch bonnet pepper, a sleek, curvaceous pod with a floral flavor and burning, loud, screeching heat. It is considered the world's hottest pepper and is treasured by connoisseurs of hot and spicy food.

For a milder sauce, substitute a jalapeño pepper for the Scotch bonnet.

½ cup dried black beans, soaked and drained
2 tablespoons vegetable oil
1 small onion, diced
1 or 2 Scotch bonnet or jalapeño peppers,
    seeded and minced
2 cloves garlic, minced
2 tablespoons red wine
1 teaspoon ground cumin
1 tablespoon minced fresh parsley
1 tablespoon fresh thyme leaves
    (or ½ teaspoon dried)
½ teaspoon salt

Place the beans in a saucepan with plenty of water and cook over medium heat for 1 hour, until the beans are tender. Drain the beans in a colander, reserving 1 cup of the cooking liquid, and set aside.

Heat the oil in a saucepan and add the onion, Scotch bonnet pepper, and garlic. Sauté for 5 to 7 minutes, until the vegetables are tender. Add the black beans, reserved cooking liquid, wine, and seasonings and simmer over medium heat for about 10 minutes.

Remove from the heat and transfer to a food processor fitted with a steel blade. Process for 15 to 20 seconds, until smooth. Transfer to a serving bowl.

Serve with tortilla chips, light sour cream, and crudités.

Yield: 1½ cups

Each serving provides:

110	Calories	13 g	Carbohydrate
4 g	Protein	185 mg	Sodium
5 g	Fat	0 mg	Cholesterol
2 g	Dietary Fiber		

Chick Pea–Tahini Guacamole

The Middle East meets the American Southwest in this creamy variation of traditional guacamole. Or is it a takeoff on hummus? You decide. Chick-a-mole! Whatever the name, you'll want to devour it. The recipe yields four servings, but if I'm in the vicinity, its more like one or two. This makes a good dip for raw or steamed vegetables.

- 2 avocadoes, peeled, pitted, and diced
- 2 cups cooked or canned chick peas, drained
- 2 medium tomatoes, cored and diced
- 1 small red onion, diced
- 2 or 3 cloves garlic, minced
- 1 or 2 jalapeño peppers, seeded and minced
- 1 tablespoon minced fresh cilantro
- ½ cup tahini (sesame paste)
- 2 tablespoons lime juice
- 1 tablespoon ground cumin
- 2 to 3 teaspoons Tabasco
      or other bottled hot sauce
- ½ teaspoon ground black pepper
- ½ teaspoon salt
- 2 scallions, finely chopped

Place all of the ingredients (except the scallions) in a food processor fitted with a steel blade. Process for 10 to 15 seconds. Stop the machine, scrape the sides, and process for another 5 seconds, or until mixture forms a chunky paste.

Scrape the dip into a serving bowl and top with the scallions. Serve with assorted vegetables, pita bread, or tortilla chips.

Yield: 4 to 6 servings

Each serving provides:

412	Calories	36 g	Carbohydrates
13 g	Protein	288 mg	Sodium
27 g	Fat	0 mg	Cholesterol
7 g	Dietary Fiber		

Spicy Peanut-Lime Dressing

This dressing embodies the flavors and ingredients of Southeast Asia: peanut butter, soy sauce, lime juice, ginger, and hot chiles. Spread it over bread, spoon it on a salad, spread it on a banana, or serve it as a vegetable dip.

½ cup chunky peanut butter
¼ cup soy sauce
3 tablespoons lime juice
2 teaspoons sesame oil
¼ cup roasted, unsalted peanuts
3 or 4 cloves garlic, minced
2 teaspoons minced ginger root
1 hot chile pepper, seeded and minced

Combine the garlic, ginger, and chile in a food processor fitted with a steel blade and process until finely chopped. Add the remaining ingredients and process until a paste is formed, stopping to scrape the side of the bowl at least once.

Serve at room temperature. If kept refrigerated, stir before serving.

Yield: 1 cup

Each serving provides:

70	Calories	3 g	Carbohydrate
3 g	Protein	297 mg	Sodium
6 g	Fat	0 mg	Cholesterol
1 g	Dietary Fiber		

Lean Bean Cuisine

Guyanese Channa

In Guyana and other parts of the Caribbean, chick peas are prepared in this way. This dish is similar to the Indian dal, *but is quicker to prepare.*

1½	tablespoons vegetable oil
1	red bell pepper, seeded and finely chopped
1	tomato, cored and chopped
4	scallions, finely chopped
1	teaspoon ground cumin
1	teaspoon ground coriander
½	teaspoon ground turmeric
½	teaspoon cayenne pepper
½	teaspoon salt
2	cups canned or cooked chick peas, drained

Heat the oil in a saucepan and add the pepper, tomato, and scallions. Cook over medium heat for 5 to 7 minutes. Blend in the seasonings and cook for 1 minute more. Stir in the chick peas and cook for about 10 minutes, mashing the peas against the side of the pan while they cook. Transfer to a serving plate and serve hot.

Yield: 4 appetizer servings

Each serving provides:

165	Calories	19 g	Carbohydrates
6 g	Protein	442 mg	Sodium
8 g	Fat	0 mg	Cholesterol
5 g	Dietary Fiber		

Dazzling International Main Dishes

If there was ever a chapter that best exemplified the new spirit of bean cookery, this one is it. Beans inspire an array of fanciful main dishes with inviting tastes, intriguing combinations, and international nuances. With this chapter (and with this book, for that matter), beans finally have a shot at the big time.

This chapter reads like a hit parade of the world's most

alluring vegetarian fare. Garden Vegetable and Black Bean Burrito, Green Lentil Curry with Potatoes and Vegetables, Mediterranean Ratatouille with Kidney Beans, Vegetable Paella with Fava Beans and Wild Rice, Thai Curried Vegetables with Adzuki Beans, and Vegetable Risotto with Cranberry Beans are a few of the globally inspired main dishes. In this nineties style of healthful-but-hearty cooking, legumes are leading the epicurean march.

And another thing: These meatless entrees are far from playing the role of meat wannabes. With the help of a strong cast of characters, including potatoes, quinoa, couscous, pumpkin, and all kinds of rices and pastas, these robust bean dishes shine on their own without the need to resemble meat-laden entrees.

As in the other chapters, a well-stocked pantry of herbs and spices is instrumental in achieving optimal flavors. Garlic, ginger, onions, sweet peppers, squash, and seasonal vegetables play an integral role as well. A penchant for the piquant helps, but is not a prerequisite. A bottle of hot sauce is always nice to have at the table.

Once again, beans prove their culinary versatility in manifold ways. Many of the dishes can be reheated the next day for lunch, or served as a side dish or cold salad.

Garden Vegetable and Black Bean Burrito

This was one of the most popular dishes at my restaurant. The vegetables and beans are rolled up in a nice, tidy package. The key is to have the flour tortillas warm and ready to be filled once the cheese is blended into the vegetables. Otherwise the heat dissolves the cheese into liquid. For a flavor jolt, add a minced jalapeño to the pan along with the vegetables.

1   tablespoon butter or oil
1   small zucchini, diced
6 to 8   mushrooms, sliced
6   broccoli florets
1   green bell pepper, seeded and diced
1   cup cooked or canned black beans
       (or any other kind), drained
½   cup corn kernels, fresh, frozen, or canned
1   teaspoon ground cumin
½ to 1   cup shredded provolone
       or Monterey jack cheese
2   (10-inch) flour tortillas, warmed

In a large skillet, melt the butter and add the zucchini, mushrooms, broccoli, and bell pepper. Sauté over medium heat for about 5 minutes, until the vegetables are tender. Reduce the heat and stir in the beans, corn, and cumin. Heat for 2 to 3 minutes more. Remove from the heat and blend in the cheese.

Place the warmed tortillas on round plates and pour some of the vegetable and cheese mixture into the center of each tortilla, forming a log. Wrap the tortillas around the vegetable mixture like a burrito or crêpe, finishing with the seam side down.

Serve with generous portions of Piquant Black Bean and Red Tomato Salsa (page 116) or your favorite salsa or guacamole.

Yield: 2 servings

Each serving provides:

583	Calories	70	g	Carbohydrate
29	g Protein	723	mg	Sodium
23	g Fat	45	mg	Cholesterol
9	g Dietary Fiber			

Lentils and Bulgur (Imjadara)

Middle Eastern food features several dishes with lentils and grains. This dish, called imjadara *(pronounced "him-jud-ruh"), was one of my Syrian grandmother's specialties. For the dish, onions are browned separately in a skillet and then stirred into the lentil and bulgur mixture. A salad of cucumbers, tomatoes, and lettuce* (insalata) *is traditionally served on the side. It leaves you feeling sated, but in a good way, like you've got energy to burn.*

1	cup dried lentils, rinsed (any kind)
4½	cups water
½	cup cracked wheat (bulgur)
½	teaspoon salt
½	teaspoon ground black pepper
2	tablespoons olive oil
1	medium onion, slivered

Combine the lentils and water in a large saucepan and bring to a simmer over medium heat. Cook for about 25 minutes, and then add the wheat, salt, and pepper. Cook for 15 minutes more, until the lentils are tender, stirring frequently. Add a little hot water if necessary.

In another skillet, heat the oil, add the onion, and sauté for 7 to 10 minutes, until browned. Stir the onions into the lentil and bulgur mixture. Serve with a tossed salad and hot pita bread.

Yield: 3 or 4 servings

Each serving provides:

299	Calories	45 g	Carbohydrate
16 g	Protein	283 mg	Sodium
8 g	Fat	0 mg	Cholesterol
9 g	Dietary Fiber		

Red Bean, Sweet Potato, and Summer Squash Gratin

This casserole dish won friends at a dish-to-pass gathering. Everyone crowded around me asking for the recipe. When compared to this dish, plain ol' mushy potatoes au gratin just don't make it. If you prefer, use soy milk or coconut milk in place of the regular milk.

3	cups diced sweet potato
2	tablespoons butter or vegetable oil
2	cups diced summer squash
2	cloves garlic, minced
4 to 6	scallions, chopped
1¼	cups milk (or coconut milk or soy milk)
1	cup cooked or canned red kidney beans or cannellini beans, drained
2	tablespoons chopped fresh basil leaves (or 2 teaspoons dried)
½	teaspoon dried thyme
½	teaspoon ground black pepper
¼	teaspoon ground cloves
¼	teaspoon salt
1	cup shredded Gouda cheese
¼	cup bread crumbs

Place the sweet potatoes in boiling water to cover and boil for about 5 minutes. Drain in a colander and cool slightly. Discard the water.

Preheat the oven to 375°F.

Melt the butter in a saucepan and add the summer squash, scallions, and garlic and sauté for 5 to 7 minutes. Add the milk, beans, and seasonings and cook over medium heat for about 5 minutes, stirring frequently.

Place the potatoes in the bottom of a lightly greased 8-inch-square casserole or gratin dish. Pour the vegetable-milk mixture over the potatoes and sprinkle with the Gouda and bread crumbs. Place in the oven and bake for 20 minutes, until a crust forms on top.

Remove from the oven and serve hot from the baking dish.

Yield: 4 servings

Each serving provides:

421	Calories	49	g	Carbohydrate
17	g Protein	541	mg	Sodium
18	g Fat	59	mg	Cholesterol
6	g Dietary Fiber			

White Bean
and Sun-Dried Tomato Risotto

Risotto is a creamy rice dish made with arborio rice, a wide Italian grain. Arborio rice, when stirred frequently, cooks to a creamy consistency and allows the essential flavors to meld together into one cohesive unit. Aside from the need to use arborio rice, there are not any strict guidelines covering the proper ingredients for a risotto. There are myriad variations; this is one of my favorites. The paprika gives it a coral hue.

10 to 12	sun-dried tomatoes
2	tablespoons butter
1	medium red onion, finely chopped
2	cloves garlic, minced
2	cups arborio rice
4	cups water
½	teaspoon paprika
¼	teaspoon ground black pepper
¼	teaspoon salt
1½	cups cooked or canned cannellini beans or small lima beans, drained
1	cup packed chopped fresh spinach
¼ to ½	cup grated Parmesan cheese

Soak the tomatoes in water to cover for 1 hour. Drain and discard the liquid. Coarsely chop the tomatoes.

In a large saucepan, melt the butter and add the onion and garlic. Sauté for 3 to 4 minutes; add the tomatoes. Sauté for 2 minutes more. Add the rice, 2 cups of the water, and seasonings and simmer uncovered for about 10 minutes, stirring frequently. Stir in the remaining 2 cups water, beans, and spinach and cook for 8 to 10 minutes more, continuing to stir, until the dish is creamy.

Turn off the heat and stir in the cheese. Serve hot.

Yield: 4 servings

Each serving provides:

587	Calories	107	g	Carbohydrate
18	g Protein	368	mg	Sodium
9	g Fat	22	mg	Cholesterol
7	g Dietary Fiber			

Vegetable Risotto
with Cranberry Beans

Risotto has become a hip dish served at many upscale restaurants. As a result, it has acquired a holier-than-thou reputation. Some chefs speak in hushed, reverent tones when discussing the esteemed risotto. To these disciples, the method of cooking is critical. It is true that risotto is prepared differently from other rice dishes: The liquid is gradually stirred into the dish, and after precisely 18 minutes the dish is carefully inspected for an optimal creamy texture. Then the cheese is delicately and expertly blended in.

It is possible, however, to prepare perfectly fine risottos without the pomp and circumstance. I have added all of the water at the beginning and let the dish simmer like an ordinary rice (but stirring it), and the result has always been tasty.

2	tablespoons butter
1	medium onion, finely chopped
6 to 8	mushrooms, sliced
2	cups arborio rice
4	cups water
1	large carrot, peeled and diced
½	teaspoon ground white pepper
½	teaspoon salt
1½	cups cooked or canned cranberry beans or pink beans
1	cup diced fresh asparagus tips
1½	cups coarsely chopped broccoli rabe leaves or spinach
¼ to ½	cup grated Parmesan cheese

In a large saucepan, melt the butter and add the onion and mushrooms. Sauté for about 5 minutes. Add the rice, 2 cups of the water, carrot, and seasonings and cook (uncovered) over medium-low heat for about 10 minutes, stirring frequently. Add the remaining 2 cups water, beans, asparagus, and broccoli rabe and cook for 8 to 10 minutes more, continuing to stir, until the dish is creamy.

Turn off the heat and stir in the cheese. Serve hot.

Yield: 4 servings

Each serving provides:

584		Calories	106	g	Carbohydrate
19	g	Protein	500	mg	Sodium
9	g	Fat	22	mg	Cholesterol
6	g	Dietary Fiber			

Summer Sauté with Pattypan Squash, Swiss Chard, and Red Beans

There is something intrinsically gratifying about taking short, squatty vegetables like pattypan squash and transforming them into an appealing, unpretentious dish. This is one of those stepping-out dishes for pattypan squash, wonderfully escorted by red beans and Swiss chard. Pampered, ritzy vegetables like white asparagus will turn green with envy. Serve this dish over cooked couscous, quinoa, or brown rice.

1 tablespoon olive oil or vegetable oil
1 tablespoon rice vinegar or wine vinegar
1 medium pattypan squash,
    large seeds removed and diced (about 2 cups)
1 red bell pepper, seeded and cut into strips
1 tablespoon minced shallots
2 cups chopped Swiss chard
1 cup cooked or canned red kidney,
    cranberry, or red chili beans, drained
2 tablespoons chopped fresh basil
2 tablespoons chopped fresh chives
¼ teaspoon ground black pepper
¼ teaspoon salt

Heat the oil and vinegar in a large skillet. Add the squash, red bell pepper, and shallots and sauté for 3 to 4 minutes. Stir in the Swiss chard and beans and cook for 2 to 3 minutes more. Stir in the herbs and seasonings and cook for 1 minute more, stirring frequently.

Remove from the heat and serve over couscous, quinoa, or brown rice. Add your favorite hot sauce at the table, or sprinkle crumbled feta cheese over the top.

Yield: 2 servings

Each serving provides:

218	Calories	30 g	Carbohydrate
10 g	Protein	353 mg	Sodium
8 g	Fat	0 mg	Cholesterol
5 g	Dietary Fiber		

Red Bean Pizza
with Mushrooms and Spinach

If you have a good pizza dough recipe, use it; otherwise a quality commercial pizza crust will do. I suggest experimenting with toppings; the variations listed at the end will give you a place to start. Pizza is a canvas, a venue to express your culinary creativity with beans. Design your own pie.

2 to 3   tablespoons olive oil
4   cloves garlic, minced
1   can (28 ounces) tomato puree
2   tablespoons dried oregano
2   tablespoons dried basil
½   teaspoon ground black pepper
½   teaspoon salt
2   cups shredded spinach
2   (12-inch) quality pizza pie shells
1   cup cooked or canned red kidney beans
     or black beans
8 to 10   mushrooms, sliced
4   cups shredded provolone or mozzarella cheese

To make the sauce, heat the oil in a saucepan and add the garlic. Cook for 5 minutes over low heat. Add the to-mato puree and seasonings and cook for 20 minutes, stirring occasionally. Stir in the spinach and cook for about 5 minutes more.

Preheat the oven to 400°F.

Lightly dust 2 baking sheets with flour and transfer the pizzas to the sheets. Ladle the sauce onto the pizza shells, spreading it evenly to the edges. Top with the beans, the mushrooms, and then the cheese. Place in the oven and bake for 15 to 20 minutes, until the crust is golden brown.

Remove the pizzas from the oven and cut into wedges.

Yield: 8 servings

Each serving provides:

507	Calories	53 g	Carbohydrate
26 g	Protein	1,391 mg	Sodium
22 g	Fat	39 mg	Cholesterol
5 g	Dietary Fiber		

Variations:
Try adding broccoli, asparagus, zucchini, goat cheese, pesto, and, of course, a variety of beans.

Black-Eyed Peas
with Bulgur and Spinach

While I was growing up, my grandmother often made this dish, which she called muir shoo shee. *But I never touched it. Not for me. Oh, if only I'd had a brain when I was a kid. Anyway, I recently rediscovered the dish in her kitchen and it was delicious. Now whenever I visit and find a pot of* muir shoo shee *sitting on the stovetop, I immediately ask for a big plate.*

This is a dish that has been passed from generation to generation but has never been written down. Until now.

2½ cups water
3 to 4 cups coarsely chopped fresh spinach
2 cups cooked or canned black-eyed peas, drained
1 cup coarse cracked wheat (bulgur)
½ teaspoon salt
½ teaspoon ground black pepper
2 tablespoons olive oil or vegetable oil
2 medium onions, sliced

In a large saucepan, bring the water to a boil. Add the spinach and peas and cook for about 5 minutes. Stir in the cracked wheat, salt, and pepper. Remove from the heat, cover, and let stand for about 15 minutes.

Meanwhile, heat the oil in a skillet and add the onions. Sauté for 7 to 10 minutes, until golden brown. Set aside.

Drain any excess water from the bulgur mixture and spoon into serving bowls. Top with the sautéed onions and serve at once.

Yield: 4 servings

Each serving provides:

322	Calories	54 g	Carbohydrate
13 g	Protein	324 mg	Sodium
8 g	Fat	0 mg	Cholesterol
17 g	Dietary Fiber		

Thai Curried Vegetables with Adzuki Beans

This dish engulfs your palate with rolling aromatic flavors accented with occasional lightning flashes of heat. The spicy nature of Thai curry paste is balanced by the smooth blend of coconut milk, soy sauce, and lime juice. Although adzuki beans are primarily used in sweet Asian dishes, they are also right at home with this entourage of ingredients.

If you can't find chayote, a tropical squash, you may substitute a small summer squash. Serve this dish over cooked jasmine rice or brown rice.

2	tablespoons vegetable oil
1	red bell pepper, seeded and cut into strips
1	chayote squash, seed removed and cut into thin strips
1	cup chopped bok choy leaves or Swiss chard leaves
6 to 8	mushrooms, sliced
1	Thai eggplant, cut into thin strips (or half a small eggplant)
1	tablespoon minced fresh ginger root
2 to 3	teaspoons Panang goong or red curry paste (available in Asian markets and specialty sections of supermarkets)
1	cup canned light coconut milk
2	tablespoons light soy sauce
1	tablespoon lime juice
1	cup cooked or canned adzuki beans or small red chili beans, drained
1	tablespoon cornstarch
1	tablespoon warm water

Heat the oil in a skillet or wok over medium heat and add the bell pepper, chayote squash, bok choy, mushrooms, and eggplant. Cook for 10 to 12 minutes, stirring occasionally. Add the ginger and curry paste and stir-fry for 1 to 2 minutes more.

Stir in the coconut milk, soy sauce, lime juice, and beans and bring to a simmer. Meanwhile, combine the cornstarch and water in a small mixing bowl. Whisk the cornstarch mixture into the coconut-curry mixture and simmer for 2 minutes more, stirring frequently.

Serve the dish with jasmine rice or brown rice.

Yield: 3 servings

Each serving provides:

374	Calories	29 g	Carbohydrate
9 g	Protein	468 mg	Sodium
27 g	Fat	0 mg	Cholesterol
3 g	Dietary Fiber		

Variation:
For an herbal nuance, stir in fresh basil leaves or chopped cilantro at the last minute.

Stuffed Roti
with Curried Chick Pea Filling

Roti (pronounced "row-tee") is a fat Caribbean sandwich stuffed with curried vegetables. Years ago, immigrant Indians brought the tradition to Trinidad, and it spread to all of the other islands. I devoured my first roti on Saint Lucia, and I was quickly converted to a roti enthusiast. Potatoes, chick peas, and pumpkin are some of my favorite fillings. Ideally, the dough should be rolled out very thin, like a samosa wrapping or a tortilla.

For the roti dough:
4	cups all-purpose flour
2	teaspoons baking powder
1	teaspoon salt
¼	cup oil

About 1 cup water

For the filling:
2	tablespoons vegetable oil
1	small red onion, diced
2	cloves garlic, minced
1	jalapeño pepper, seeded and minced
1½	tablespoons curry powder
1	teaspoon ground coriander or cumin
¼	teaspoon salt
4	cups diced white potatoes, sweet potatoes, or winter squash
1¼	cups water
2	cups cooked or canned chick peas, drained
1	tablespoon butter

To make the dough, combine the dry ingredients in a mixing bowl. Gradually add the oil and water to the bowl, mixing and kneading the dough as you go. The dough should not be so wet that it sticks to your fingers, but should hold together when pressed into a ball. Form a ball and set the dough aside for about 15 minutes.

To make the filling, heat the oil in a skillet and add the onion, garlic, and jalapeño. Sauté for 4 to 5 minutes over medium heat. Add the seasonings and cook 1 minute more. Add the potato and water and cook for about 15 minutes, until the potatoes are tender.

Add the chick peas and cook for another 5 to 10 minutes, until the filling is chunky and thick. Set the filling aside.

Divide the dough into 4 to 6 equal-sized balls. Flatten each ball and roll out into thin 8-inch squares. Fill the middle of each square with about ½ cup of the filling. Wrap the dough around the mixture, burrito style, and seal the filling inside.

To cook the roti, heat the butter in a skillet over high heat until it sizzles. Reduce the heat to medium and, using a large spatula, place a filled roti in the pan. Cook for 3 to 4 minutes, until the crust is golden brown. Turn with a wide spatula and continue cooking. Repeat the process with the remaining roti. Serve the roti with your favorite hot sauce.

Yield: 4 large servings

Each serving provides:

939	Calories	150 g	Carbohydrate
24 g	Protein	981 mg	Sodium
27 g	Fat	8 mg	Cholesterol
10 g	Dietary Fiber		

Creole Veggie
and Red Bean Jambalaya

This was a premier vegetarian dish on my restaurant's menu.

Jambalaya is a hearty Creole dish of rice, vegetables, and hot and spicy seasonings. It has traditionally included meat, but this version retains the spirit and heartiness of the original jambalaya while jettisoning the meat.

For the Creole sauce:
1½ tablespoons vegetable oil
1   small green bell pepper, seeded and diced
1   small onion, diced
½   cup diced celery
½   cup diced okra
2   cloves garlic, minced
2   cups canned crushed tomatoes
¾   cup water or vegetable stock
2   tablespoons dry red wine
1   tablespoon dried oregano
1   teaspoon dried parsley
1   teaspoon dried thyme
1 to 2   teaspoons Tabasco
    or other bottled hot sauce
¼   teaspoon salt
¼   teaspoon ground black pepper
⅛   teaspoon ground cayenne pepper

For the vegetables:
2   tablespoons butter or vegetable oil
2   green bell peppers, seeded and diced
12 to 16   mushrooms, sliced
12   broccoli florets

1	small zucchini, diced
1	cup cooked or canned red kidney beans or black beans, drained
½	cup corn kernels, fresh, frozen, or canned
6	cups cooked white or brown rice

To make the sauce, heat the oil in a large saucepan and add the green pepper, onion, celery, okra, and garlic. Cook over medium heat for about 10 minutes, stirring occasionally.

Reduce heat to medium-low and add the tomatoes, water, wine, and seasonings. Cook for 20 to 25 minutes, stirring occasionally. Reduce the heat as the sauce thickens. Set aside.

To make the vegetables, heat the butter in a large skillet over medium heat and add all of the vegetables except the beans and corn. Cook for 7 to 10 minutes, until the vegetables are tender, stirring occasionally. Add the beans, corn, and Creole sauce to the pan and bring to a simmer. Continue to cook for 3 to 4 minutes, stirring frequently.

Place 1½ cups of the cooked rice in the center of each plate and pour the Creole vegetables over it. Serve hot.

Yield: 4 large servings

Each serving provides:

669	Calories	121 g	Carbohydrate
19 g	Protein	448 mg	Sodium
13 g	Fat	16 mg	Cholesterol
9 g	Dietary Fiber		

Variation:
Sprinkle shredded provolone cheese on top before serving.

Two-Bean, Two-Cheese Lasagna with Leafy Green Vegetables

If you have ever been traumatized by cafeteria-style, greasy lasagna bloated with meat, this dish is the proper therapy. Beans are a natural in this savory, cheesy lasagna filled with leafy greens and herbal seasonings.

2   tablespoons olive oil
1   medium onion, finely chopped
4   cloves garlic, minced
1   can (28 ounces) tomato puree
2   tomatoes, cored and diced
1   cup cooked or canned pink or red beans, drained
2   tablespoons dried oregano
1   tablespoon dried basil
1   teaspoon ground black pepper
½   teaspoon salt
12 to 14   uncooked lasagna noodles
2 to 3   cups ricotta cheese
2   cups cooked or canned navy beans
      or other small white beans, drained
1   egg, beaten
2   cups finely chopped mustard greens,
      spinach, or Swiss chard
2   tablespoons minced fresh parsley
2½ to 3   cups shredded mozzarella cheese

Heat the oil in a medium saucepan and add the onion and garlic. Cook for 5 to 7 minutes over medium heat. Add the tomato puree, tomatoes, pink beans, and seasonings and cook for 30 minutes, stirring occasionally.

To parboil the lasagna noodles, place 7 or 8 noodles at a time into boiling water to cover and cook for 4 to 6 minutes. Stir occasionally to keep the noodles from sticking together. Remove with a slotted spoon and rinse in cold water. Store the lasagna strips in a single layer on waxed paper.

Preheat the oven to 375°F.

In a mixing bowl, combine the ricotta cheese, white beans, egg, greens, and parsley.

Spread a little sauce in the bottom of a 9- by 13-inch pan. Cover with a third of the noodles, then half of the ricotta-bean mixture. Spread a third of the sauce over the mixture, sprinkle half of the mozzarella over it, then cover with more noodles. Repeat the layering process with half the remaining sauce, the rest of the ricotta mixture, and the rest of the noodles. Finish with the remaining sauce on top and then sprinkle with the remaining mozzarella.

Bake for 30 to 40 minutes. Let cool for 10 minutes before serving. Cut into rectangles and serve with Italian bread.

Yield: 10 to 12 servings

Each serving provides:

474	Calories	56 g	Carbohydrate
25 g	Protein	555 mg	Sodium
17 g	Fat	70 mg	Cholesterol
6 g	Dietary Fiber		

Moroccan Fava Bean and Winter Squash Stew

This is a dish I make for really close friends, because I tend to eat it right out of the pot. The recipe yields four servings, but in front of me, it yields one. It is that good. For the squash, I like to use jack-o'-lantern pumpkin when it is in season; otherwise, any winter squash will do. Harissa, a Moroccan spice paste, is available in the specialty sections of most supermarkets. The leftovers, if there are any, can be used as a salad the next day.

2   tablespoons vegetable oil or olive oil
1   large onion, diced
1   red bell pepper, seeded and diced
1   tomato, cored and diced
3 or 4   cloves garlic, minced
2   cups water
2   cups diced pumpkin or butternut or acorn squash
1   cup cooked or canned small fava
       or cranberry beans, drained
1   cup cooked or canned chick peas, drained
2   tablespoons minced fresh parsley
2   tablespoons harissa (Moroccan chile paste)
1   cup couscous

Heat the oil in a skillet and add the onion and bell pepper. Sauté for about 5 minutes. Add the tomato and garlic and cook for 4 minutes more. Stir in the remaining ingredients (except the couscous) and cook for 30 minutes over medium heat, until the squash is tender. Stir occasionally.

Stir in the couscous, cover, and let sit for 10 minutes. Serve hot.

Yield: 4 servings

Each serving provides:

438	Calories	69	g	Carbohydrate
15 g	Protein	17	mg	Sodium
12 g	Fat	0	mg	Cholesterol
7 g	Dietary Fiber			

Variation:
In lieu of harissa, try a combination of cumin, cayenne pepper, coriander, and salt to taste.

Vegetable Paella with Fava Beans and Wild Rice

Paella roughly means "pan" in Spanish, but it might as well mean "abundance" or "eat with gusto." With this in mind, I have retained the spirit of classic paella while creating a meatless version. It overflows with a bounty of vegetables and beans. Wild rice, which is not really rice at all but the seed of a native American aquatic grass (you knew that), adds a crunchy texture and earthy flavor.

2 to 3   tablespoons olive oil
1   large onion, diced
1   green or red bell pepper, seeded and diced
1   unpeeled yellow squash, diced
10 to 12   mushrooms, sliced
3 or 4   cloves garlic, minced
3/4   teaspoon ground turmeric or a pinch of saffron
2½   cups water or vegetable stock
2   cups cooked or canned small fava
         or red kidney beans, drained
2   carrots, peeled and diced
1   cup green peas, fresh or frozen
1   cup medium-grain brown rice
½   cup wild rice
1   tablespoon fresh thyme leaves
         (or 1 teaspoon dried)
1   teaspoon ground black pepper

Preheat the oven to 350°F.

In a large flameproof casserole or Dutch oven, heat the oil and add the onion, pepper, squash, mushrooms, and garlic. Cook over medium heat for 7 to 10 minutes. Add the turmeric and cook 1 minute more. Stir in the water, beans, carrots, green peas, both rices, and seasonings, and cover.

Place in the oven and bake for 55 minutes to 1 hour, until the rice is done.

Fluff the paella and serve hot. Season with salt at the table.

Yield: 4 servings

Each serving provides:

521	Calories	90 g	Carbohydrate
19 g	Protein	30 mg	Sodium
11 g	Fat	0 mg	Cholesterol
12 g	Dietary Fiber		

Variation:

After baking for 50 minutes, add 10 to 12 asparagus stalks, sliced ¾ inch thick, or broccoli florets to the paella. Cover and continue to cook. Or add 1 cup of corn kernels in place of the green peas.

Southern Tureen
of Black-Eyed Peas,
Collard Greens, and Yams

For this dish, the marquee ingredients of Southern food appear in a slightly different guise. They are all simmered together in one big pot. The result is a nourishing, healthful meal. Salt pork and bacon were not invited to this show.

2   tablespoons vegetable oil
1   large red onion, slivered
4   cups chopped collard greens (about a half bunch)
2   cups diced yams or sweet potatoes (do not peel)
2   cups cooked or canned black-eyed peas, drained
2   cups water
½   teaspoon ground black pepper
½   teaspoon salt
2   tablespoons yellow cornmeal (optional)

Heat the oil in a large flameproof casserole or Dutch oven. Add the onion and cook for about 8 minutes, stirring occasionally, until lightly browned. Add the collard greens, yams, black-eyed peas, water, pepper, and salt, and cover. Bring to a simmer and cook for about 20 minutes, stirring ocassionally.

To thicken, gradually stir in the cornmeal and cook for 5 to 10 minutes more. Serve in large tureens or bowls, with corn bread.

Yield: 4 servings

Each serving provides:

283	Calories	47	g	Carbohydrate
9	g Protein	297	mg	Sodium
8	g Fat	0	mg	Cholesterol
13	g Dietary Fiber			

Green Lentil Curry
with Potatoes and Vegetables

Green lentils are quite abundant in India and are rapidly becoming more available in the United States. The lentils form a natural alliance with the deep, pungent flavors of Indian curry. You can also use green mung beans for this dish as well as other kinds of lentils. Cucumber Raita (page 208) or plain lowfat yogurt make a soothing accompaniment. Serve it over basmati rice.

2 cups dried green, red, or brown lentils, rinsed
2 tablespoons vegetable oil
1 medium onion, diced
10 to 12 mushrooms, sliced
1 small zucchini, diced
2 tomatoes, cored and diced
3 or 4 cloves garlic, minced
1 jalapeño pepper, seeded and minced (optional)
1 tablespoon minced fresh ginger root
1 tablespoon Madras
   or Caribbean-style curry powder
1 teaspoon ground cumin
1 teaspoon ground coriander or garam masala
1 teaspoon salt
½ teaspoon ground black pepper
2 cups unpeeled, diced white potatoes
2 carrots, peeled and diced
8 broccoli or cauliflower florets

Place the lentils in plenty of water to cover and cook for about 45 minutes, until tender. Drain the lentils in a colander, reserving 2 cups of the cooking liquid, and set aside.

Heat the oil in a large saucepan over medium heat and add the onion, mushrooms, and zucchini. Cook for about 7 minutes, until the vegetables are tender, stirring occasionally. Add the tomatoes, garlic, jalapeño, and ginger, and cook for 4 to 5 minutes more. Add the seasonings and cook 1 minute more.

Blend in the lentils, reserved cooking liquid, potatoes, and carrots and cook over low heat for 35 to 40 minutes, stirring occasionally. Add the broccoli and cook for another 5 to 10 minutes.

Remove from the heat and serve with basmati rice.

Yield: 6 to 8 servings

Each serving provides:

303	Calories		49 g	Carbohydrate
19 g	Protein		342 mg	Sodium
5 g	Fat		0 mg	Cholesterol
10 g	Dietary Fiber			

Jessica's Sweet-and-Sour Lentils

This recipe was prompted by my friend Jessica, who had been reminiscing about her Peace Corps days in Bolivia. Her description of the lack of protein in the volunteers' diets, their small budget, and their yearning for take-out food inspired us to create this improvised dish of sweet-and-sour lentils. Serve it over cooked white rice.

1   cup brown lentils, rinsed
2   tablespoons vegetable oil
1   medium onion, chopped
1   red or green bell pepper, seeded and diced
1   zucchini, diced
1   can (10 ounces) pineapple chunks
      (or 2 cups fresh)
2   tablespoons minced fresh ginger root
¼   cup red wine vinegar or rice vinegar
2   tablespoons dry sherry
2   tablespoons light soy sauce
2   tablespoons brown sugar
2   tablespoons catsup
2 to 3   teaspoons Tabasco
      or other bottled hot sauce
½   teaspoon ground black pepper
1   teaspoon cornstarch

Place the lentils in water to cover and cook for about 45 minutes, until tender. Drain the lentils in a colander.

In a large saucepan, heat the oil and add the onion, green pepper, and zucchini. Sauté for 7 minutes; add the pineapple and ginger and cook for 2 to 3 minutes more. Add the lentils, vinegar, sherry, soy sauce, sugar, catsup, hot sauce, and pepper and cook over medium heat for 15 to 20 minutes, stirring occasionally.

Combine the cornstarch with an equal amount of warm water in a small bowl. Whisk the cornstarch mixture into the lentils, reduce the heat, and cook for 5 to 10 minutes more.

Serve over white rice.

Yield: 4 servings

Each serving provides:

342	Calories	57	g	Carbohydrate
16	g Protein	423	mg	Sodium
8	g Fat	0	mg	Cholesterol
7	g Dietary Fiber			

Quinoa Stir-Fry
with Beans, Pineapple,
and Asian Vegetables

Merging ethnic cuisines opens up a window and an array of new and exciting flavors come into view. For this dish, cranberry beans and quinoa of South America meet the stir-fried vegetables and spices of Asia. The result is a delectable trans-Pacific union of tastes.

2   cups quinoa, rinsed
4   cups water
2   tablespoons peanut oil or vegetable oil
1   chayote squash or small zucchini,
     peeled and cut into matchsticks
1   red bell pepper, seeded and slivered
6 to 8   mushrooms, sliced
1   (2- to 4-inch-long) daikon (Japanese radish),
     thinly sliced into discs
1   cup diced pineapple, fresh or canned
1   tablespoon minced fresh ginger root
⅓   cup light soy sauce
1   tablespoon lime juice
1   teaspoon dark sesame oil
1   teaspoon hot sesame oil or Tabasco
     or other bottled hot sauce
1   tablespoon cornstarch
1   cup cooked or canned cranberry beans
     or black beans, drained
1   cup bean sprouts
1   cup shredded bok choy leaves or Chinese cabbage
4   scallions, finely chopped

Place the quinoa and water in a saucepan and bring to a simmer. Cover and cook over low heat until all of the water is absorbed, about 15 minutes. Set aside and keep warm.

In a wok or skillet, heat the peanut oil until it sizzles. Add the squash, bell pepper, mushrooms, and daikon and cook for 5 to 7 minutes, stirring frequently. Stir in the pineapple and ginger and stir-fry for 3 to 4 minutes more.

Stir in the soy sauce, lime juice, and sesame oils and bring to a simmer. Combine the cornstarch with an equal amount of water and whisk into the mixture. Follow with the beans, bean sprouts, and bok choy, return to a simmer, and simmer for 2 to 3 minutes more.

Transfer the quinoa to warm plates and serve the stir-fried vegetables and beans over the top. Top each dish with the scallions.

Yield: 4 servings

Each serving provides:

535	Calories	86 g	Carbohydrates
19 g	Protein	857 mg	Sodium
15 g	Fat	0 mg	Cholesterol
15 g	Dietary Fiber		

Pasta
with Garden Tomato Sauce,
Red Beans, and Feta

*Once you try this sauce, you won't ever want to stand in line
at some trendy trattoria waiting to pay outlandish prices for a
pompous pasta dish with an unpronounceable, faddish name
and weird shape. This is a simple, unpretentious dish. The feta
and parsley sprinkled over the brilliant red sauce make a pretty
picture.*

2 to 3 tablespoons olive oil
1 medium onion, chopped
4 cloves garlic, minced
3 large, ripe tomatoes
    or 6 plum tomatoes, cored and diced
1 medium zucchini, diced
1 tablespoon dried oregano
1 tablespoon dried basil
1 tablespoon sugar
1 teaspoon salt
¼ teaspoon ground cayenne pepper
1 can (28 ounces) tomato puree
2 cups cooked or canned red kidney beans
    or cranberry beans, drained
1 pound uncooked pasta shells, spirals, or linguini
⅓ pound crumbled feta cheese
2 tablespoons minced fresh parsley

Heat the oil in a saucepan and add the onion and garlic. Sauté for about 5 minutes, until tender. Add the fresh tomatoes, zucchini, and seasonings and cook for about 10 minutes on medium-low heat. Stir in the tomato puree and beans and simmer for 25 to 30 minutes, stirring occasionally.

Meanwhile, place the pasta in boiling water to cover, stir, and return to a boil. Cook, uncovered, for 9 to 12 minutes, until the pasta is al dente. Drain in a colander and keep warm. (If the pasta sticks together, run hot water over it in the colander.)

When the sauce is done, transfer the pasta to serving bowls and ladle the sauce over the top. Sprinkle the cheese and parsley over the sauce. Serve with Italian garlic bread.

Yield: 6 servings

Each serving provides:

569	Calories	94 g	Carbohydrate
22 g	Protein	1,188 mg	Sodium
13 g	Fat	22 mg	Cholesterol
8 g	Dietary Fiber		

Brazilian Vegetarian Feijoada with Black Beans

The challenge here was to create a meatless dish while retaining the distinctive smoky quality of feijoada *(pronounced "fay-zhwa-duh"), the Brazilian national dish. The answer was to use a smidgen of liquid smoke, a prominent ingredient in commercial barbecue sauces. If you have an aversion to liquid smoke, try adding a chipotle pepper.*

1	cup black beans, soaked and drained
2	tablespoons vegetable oil
1	large onion, chopped
1	large red bell pepper, seeded and diced
1	large tomato, cored and diced
4	cloves garlic, minced
1	small jalapeño pepper, seeded and minced
1	tablespoon rice vinegar or red wine vinegar
1½	teaspoons ground cumin
1	tablespoon fresh thyme leaves (or 1 teaspoon dried)
1	teaspoon salt
½	teaspoon ground black pepper
½	teaspoon bottled liquid smoke
2	tablespoons minced fresh parsley
4 to 6	cups cooked white rice

Place the beans in plenty of water and cook for 1 hour, until tender. Drain, reserving 1¼ cups of the cooking liquid, and set aside.

Heat the oil in a large saucepan and add the onion and bell pepper. Sauté for about 5 minutes. Add the tomato, garlic, and jalapeño and cook for 4 minutes more.

Add the beans, reserved cooking liquid, vinegar, all of the seasonings (except the parsley), and liquid smoke and cook for 30 to 40 minutes over medium heat, stirring occasionally. The mixture should be thick and chunky.

Ladle the feijoada into large bowls and sprinkle with parsley. Serve with the rice.

Yield: 4 to 6 servings

Each serving provides:

483	Calories	90 g	Carbohydrate
15 g	Protein	453 mg	Sodium
7 g	Fat	0 mg	Cholesterol
7 g	Dietary Fiber		

Variation:
For an impressive presentation, stir in about 1 cup of chopped spinach a few minutes before serving. The verdant spinach balances the dark hue of the molten black beans.

Mediterranean Ratatouille with Kidney Beans

Ratatouille is the quintessential eggplant dish. It doesn't disguise the eggplant's true flavor, as breading and frying tends to do. Red kidney beans make a natural ingredient for this hearty vegetarian stew-meal. Serve it over cooked rice or pasta.

If you have an aversion to cooking eggplant in its natural state (some people detect bitterness—I don't), place it in a sieve and sprinkle with salt. Let stand for 20 minutes before adding to the recipe.

2	tablespoons vegetable oil
1	large onion, slivered
4	cloves garlic, minced
1	green or red bell pepper, seeded and chopped
4	cups diced eggplant (do not peel)
1	small summer squash, diced
4	ripe tomatoes, cored and diced
1	tablespoon dried basil
1	tablespoon dried oregano
1	teaspoon salt
¼	teaspoon ground cayenne pepper
2	cups cooked or canned red kidney beans, drained
½ to 1	cup grated Parmesan or Romano cheese

Heat the oil in a large saucepan and add the onion. Sauté for 5 minutes. Add all of the remaining ingredients (except the beans and cheese) and cook over medium-low heat for 15 minutes, stirring occasionally.

Stir in the beans and cook for 15 to 20 minutes more, stirring occasionally. Sprinkle with the cheese and serve over rice or pasta.

Yield: 4 to 6 servings

Each serving provides:

265	Calories	33 g	Carbohydrates
14 g	Protein	679 mg	Sodium
10 g	Fat	9 mg	Cholesterol
6 g	Dietary Fiber		

Chilean Pumpkin Stew with Corn and Beans

This flavorful vegetable stew has roots in the native Indian cooking of South America. Chileans would use calabaza pumpkin, but the jack-o'-lantern pumpkin or other winter squash can be used. The meal could easily have been prepared by native North Americans, since pumpkin, corn, and beans are indigenous to North America as well. Chileans like to serve it with a spicy, salsalike condiment called pebre.

1	cup cranberry, anasazi, or pink beans, soaked and drained
2	tablespoons vegetable oil
1	large onion, diced
2 or 3	cloves garlic, minced
1½	tablespoons paprika
4	large tomatoes, cored and diced
2	teaspoons dried oregano
¾	teaspoon salt
½	teaspoon ground black pepper
2	cups peeled, chopped pumpkin or butternut squash
1	cup corn kernels, fresh, frozen, or canned

Place the beans in a saucepan, add plenty of water to cover, and cook for 1 to 1½ hours, until the beans are tender. Drain, reserving 1½ cups of the cooking liquid, and set aside.

In a large saucepan, heat the oil and add the onion, garlic, and paprika and sauté for about 5 minutes. Add the tomatoes and seasonings and cook for about 10 minutes more, until the mixture is a thick pulp. Add the beans, reserved cooking liquid, and squash and cook for 15 to 20 minutes, stirring occasionally, until the squash is tender. Stir in the corn and return to a simmer for a few minutes.

Serve the stew in bowls with rice on the side.

Yield: 4 servings

Each serving provides:

344	Calories	56 g	Carbohydrate
16 g	Protein	438 mg	Sodium
9 g	Fat	0 mg	Cholesterol
10 g	Dietary Fiber		

Sri Lankan Sambar with Coconut-Cilantro Chutney (Lentil and Vegetable Curry)

Sambar is a spicy curried dish of lentils and vegetables often served with chutney. I like to devour this dish with tandem eating strokes: first, a bite of the curry, then a taste of the chutney, then a mouthful of the curry, then back to the chutney, and so forth. And about that fast. That way the flavors form the most pleasurable unison possible. Serve the curry over rice.

For the chutney:
1   cup shredded coconut (unsweetened, if possible)
¼   cup finely chopped cilantro
1   tablespoon minced fresh ginger root
1   teaspoon paprika
½   teaspoon salt
¼   teaspoon ground cayenne pepper
½   cup plain yogurt
1   teaspoon lemon juice

For the sambar:
1   cup yellow or red lentils or split peas, rinsed
5   cups water
1   medium onion, diced
2   cloves garlic, minced
1   large tomato, cored and diced
1   tablespoon Madras or other quality curry powder
½   teaspoon ground coriander
½   teaspoon ground black pepper
½   teaspoon salt
¼   teaspoon ground turmeric
2   carrots, peeled and diced

1   cup chopped white potato or other tuber
4 to 6   cups cooked white rice, preferably basmati

Combine all of the chutney ingredients in a mixing bowl and blend well. Transfer to a serving bowl and chill for 1 hour.

To make the sambar, place the lentils and water in a saucepan and cook for about 45 minutes, until tender. Drain, reserving 1 cup of the cooking liquid, and set aside. Heat the oil in a large skillet and add the onion and garlic. Sauté for 5 minutes. Add the tomato and cook for 5 minutes more. Stir in the seasonings and cook for an additional minute. Add the carrots, potato, lentils, and reserved cooking liquid and cook for about 20 minutes over medium-low heat.

Serve the lentil curry over rice with the chutney on the side.

Yield: 4 servings

Each serving provides:

697		Calories	122	g	Carbohydrate
25	g	Protein	597	mg	Sodium
13	g	Fat	4	mg	Cholesterol
11	g	Dietary Fiber			

Curried Autumn Pumpkin and Red Beans

I have long bemoaned the fact that pumpkins are so often typecast as material for pie or, worse, as stoop ornaments or doorstops. No more. I am on a mission to trumpet the many virtues of this versatile autumn squash. It is filled with beta carotene and other nutrients, and deserves more respect than it gets. Here is a dish that elevates the humble pumpkin to gourmet status, with a little help from beans. Basmati or jasmine rice makes a nice accompaniment.

To prepare the pumpkin, cut it in half, remove the seeds, and peel the outer skin off. To make the peeling process easier, some folks recommend parboiling or baking the pumpkin first.

2	tablespoons vegetable oil
4	cups peeled, diced pumpkin
2	medium onions, diced
2	tomatoes, cored and chopped
4	cloves garlic, minced
1	tablespoon minced fresh ginger root
1½	tablespoons curry powder
2	tablespoons minced fresh parsley
2	teaspoons ground cumin
½	teaspoon ground black pepper
½	teaspoon salt
¼	teaspoon ground cloves
2	cups water
2	cups cooked or canned red kidney beans, drained

Heat the oil in a large saucepan and add the pumpkin and onion. Cook over medium heat for 4 minutes, stirring occasionally. Add the tomatoes, garlic, and ginger, and cook for 4 minutes more. Add the seasonings and cook for 1 minute more, stirring frequently. Stir in the water and cook for 35 to 45 minutes, until the pumpkin is tender. Stir in the beans and cook for about 10 minutes more over low heat.

Remove from the heat and serve with basmati or jasmine rice.

Yield: 4 to 6 servings

Each serving provides:

222	Calories	35 g	Carbohydrate
9 g	Protein	232 mg	Sodium
7 g	Fat	0 mg	Cholesterol
7 g	Dietary Fiber		

Winter Squash
Stuffed with White Beans
and Wheat Berries

This dish radiates with healthful vibrations and tastes. Two nutritious stalwarts, beans and squash, are joined by wheat berries, another nutritional powerhouse. Like beans, wheat berries (also called wheat kernels) should be soaked overnight before cooking. Wheat berries can be found at natural food stores and in the specialty section of some supermarkets.

1	cup wheat berries, soaked and drained
3	cups water
2	delicata, acorn, or butternut squash
2	cups cooked or canned navy beans or other small white beans, drained
3 to 4	tablespoons olive oil
2 or 3	cloves garlic, minced
2	tablespoons minced fresh parsley
1	teaspoon onion powder
1/2	teaspoon dried thyme
1/2	teaspoon ground allspice
1/2	teaspoon ground black pepper
1/2	teaspoon salt

Combine the wheat berries and water in a saucepan and bring to a boil. Simmer for 1½ to 2 hours, until tender. Drain in a colander and return to the pan.

Meanwhile, preheat the oven to 350°F. Cut the squash in half lengthwise and remove the seeds. Place flesh side down in a baking pan with about ¼ inch of water. Place in oven and bake for 35 to 45 minutes, until tender. Remove and keep warm.

Add the beans, olive oil, garlic, and seasonings to the pan containing the cooked wheat berries. Cook over low heat for about 10 minutes, stirring occasionally.

Arrange the squash on serving plates. Fill with the bean–wheat berry mixture and serve at once. Refrigerate any remaining bean-berry mixture and serve as a salad the next day.

Yield: 4 servings

Each serving provides:

491	Calories	82 g	Carbohydrate
16 g	Protein	288 mg	Sodium
14 g	Fat	0 mg	Cholesterol
12 g	Dietary Fiber		

Splendid
Side Dishes

From the classic well-fried beans and baked beans to the traditional staple of red beans and rice, all kinds of beans are at home in the role of a side dish. In this chapter, many of the conventional dishes have been rescued from the dominance of meat and are new and improved versions perfect for our times. Today's side dishes of beans are often lighter, less fatty, and more healthful than their predecessors.

The recipes in this chapter exude the panache and flair usually expected of headlining main dishes; the only difference is that they are served in smaller portions. Succotash with Cranberry Beans and Chiles, Rustic Well-Fried Beans, Caribbean Rice and Peas, Spiced Aromatic Lentils with Cucumber Raita, Pumpkin Rice with Gungo Peas, Stovetop Beans with Sweet Potatoes, and Chipotle Baked Campfire Beans are some of the appealing side-of-the-plate selections that await you. Many of these side dishes even come close to stealing the show from the main dish.

For newcomers to bean cuisine, this chapter offers plenty of places to cut in to the big dance of bean cookery without a lot of effort or practice. Recipes such as Beans for Beginners, Red Chili Beans and Couscous, and Red Beans and Brown Rice are easy-to-prepare dishes designed for entry-level cooks. These dishes are far more rewarding than eating beans out of a can or having no beans at all, but they do not involve an elaborate production.

Succotash
with Cranberry Beans
and Chiles

A variety of beans can be used in succotash, the culinary marriage of corn and beans. For this spicy version, I've added cranberry beans, chiles, and oregano.

1½ cups frozen Green Fordhook lima beans
1 tablespoon vegetable oil
4 scallions, chopped
1 red bell pepper, seeded and diced
2 cloves garlic, minced
1 jalapeño pepper or red Fresno pepper,
   seeded and minced
1½ cups corn kernels, fresh, frozen, or canned
1 cup cooked or canned cranberry, anasazi,
   or pink beans, drained
2 teaspoons dried oregano
½ teaspoon ground black pepper
½ teaspoon salt

Place the lima beans in boiling water to cover and cook for 8 to 10 minutes, until tender. Drain, discarding the liquid, and set aside.

Heat the oil in a saucepan and add the scallions, bell pepper, garlic, and jalapeño pepper. Sauté for about 7 minutes, then add the corn, cranberry beans, lima beans, and seasonings. Cook for about 10 minutes more, stirring occasionally.

Transfer the succotash to serving bowls and serve hot. For an extra kick, pass the Tabasco or other bottled hot sauce at the table.

Yield: 4 servings

Each serving provides:

220	Calories	37	g	Carbohydrate
11	g Protein	321	mg	Sodium
5	g Fat	0	mg	Cholesterol
12	g Dietary Fiber			

Variation:
Blend in smooth goat cheese and minced cilantro or basil at the last minute.

Caribbean Rice and Peas

Rice and peas, a Caribbean staple, is prepared in a variety of ways throughout the islands. Some islanders use kidney beans, others use pigeon peas or cow peas. ("Peas" can refer to either beans or peas.) Although traditional recipes call for chicken or ham, substituting water or vegetable stock is the way to go. A touch of coconut milk gives the dish a sweet, nutty nuance and authentic flavor.

2	tablespoons vegetable oil
1	small onion, diced
1	carrot, peeled and diced
2	cloves garlic, minced
1	Scotch bonnet pepper or other chile pepper, seeded and minced
1½	cups uncooked white long-grain rice
2	cups water or vegetable stock
1	cup canned coconut milk
1½	cups cooked or canned red kidney beans or pigeon peas, drained
2	teaspoons fresh thyme leaves (or ½ teaspoon dried)
¼	teaspoon ground allspice
¼	teaspoon ground black pepper
¼	teaspoon salt

Heat the oil in a saucepan and add the onion, carrot, garlic, and Scotch bonnet pepper. Sauté over medium heat for about 7 minutes. Stir in the rice, water, coconut milk, beans, and seasonings. Cover and cook over medium heat for 15 to 20 minutes. When the rice is done, transfer to a serving bowl. Fluff the rice and serve hot.

Yield: 4 servings

Each serving provides:

532	Calories	77	g	Carbohydrate
12 g	Protein	155	mg	Sodium
20 g	Fat	0	mg	Cholesterol
4 g	Dietary Fiber			

Pumpkin Rice
with Gungo Peas

I was vacationing on Saint Martins when I tasted this savory dish of calabaza (West Indian pumpkin), gungo peas, and rice. My perception of pumpkin was forever changed. Pumpkins in paradise? Absolutely. This side dish became a popular autumn special at my restaurant. You can substitute the familiar jack-o'-lantern pumpkin or butternut squash for the calabaza.

2	tablespoons vegetable oil
1	medium onion, diced
2	cups diced calabaza (West Indian pumpkin), pumpkin, or butternut squash
½	Scotch bonnet pepper or 1 jalapeño pepper, seeded and minced
4	cloves garlic, minced
1	tablespoon minced fresh ginger root
1½	tablespoons curry powder
1	teaspoon ground cumin
½	teaspoon ground cloves
½	teaspoon ground allspice
½	teaspoon ground black pepper
½	teaspoon salt
4	cups water
2	cups uncooked white rice
1	cup cooked or canned gungo peas (pigeon peas) or small red chili beans, drained
2	cups coarsely chopped kale or spinach

In a saucepan, heat the oil and add the onion, calabaza, chile pepper, garlic, and ginger. Sauté for 5 to 7 minutes, until the onions are tender. Add the seasonings and cook for 1 minute more. Add the water and rice and cover. Simmer over medium heat for about 15 minutes. Stir in the gungo peas and kale, cover, and cook over low heat for about 5 minutes more, until the rice is done and the pumpkin is tender.

Fluff the rice and serve hot.

Yield: 6 to 8 servings

Each serving provides:

297	Calories	57	g	Carbohydrate
7	g Protein	172	mg	Sodium
5	g Fat	0	mg	Cholesterol
4	g Dietary Fiber			

Red Beans and Brown Rice

Here is a healthful spin on the classic Louisiana dish. This version is meatless but twice as flavorful. The secret is the well-balanced blend of seasonings. Brown rice has more fiber than white rice and a chewier texture because the bran is still intact.

2	tablespoons vegetable oil
1	medium onion, diced
1	green bell pepper, seeded and diced
3 or 4	cloves garlic, minced
1½	cups uncooked brown rice
3¼	cups water or vegetable stock
2	teaspoons dried oregano
1 to 3	teaspoons Tabasco or other bottled hot sauce
1	teaspoon dried thyme
1	teaspoon salt
½	teaspoon ground black pepper
¼	teaspoon ground cayenne pepper
¼	teaspoon ground white pepper
2	cups cooked or canned red kidney beans, drained
2	medium carrots, peeled and diced

Heat the oil in a saucepan and add the onion, bell pepper, and garlic. Sauté for 5 to 7 minutes, until the vegetables are tender. Add the rice, water, and seasonings. Cover and cook over medium heat for 30 minutes. Add the beans and carrots, cover, and cook for 15 minutes more, until the rice has absorbed all of the water.

Fluff the rice and let stand for 10 minutes before serving.

Yield: 4 to 6 servings

Each serving provides:

380	Calories	67 g	Carbohydrate
12 g	Protein	471 mg	Sodium
8 g	Fat	0 mg	Cholesterol
6 g	Dietary Fiber		

Stovetop Beans
with Sweet Potatoes

For this dish, the flavors of baked beans are enriched with beta carotene–rich sweet potatoes. Although this dish is traditionally baked, it also cooks up nicely on the stovetop.

1   cup dried pinto beans or navy beans
      or other small white beans, soaked and drained
3   cups diced sweet potatoes (do not peel)
2   tablespoons vegetable oil
1   medium onion, diced
1   red bell pepper, seeded and diced
2   cloves garlic, minced
½   cup catsup or mango chutney
⅓   cup molasses
3   tablespoons Worcestershire sauce
2   teaspoons chili powder
1   teaspoon ground cumin
1   teaspoon Tabasco or other bottled hot sauce
½   teaspoon ground black pepper
½   teaspoon salt

Place the beans in a saucepan with plenty of water to cover and cook for 1 hour over medium heat. Drain the beans, discarding the liquid, and set aside.

Place the potatoes in boiling water to cover and cook for 10 minutes. Drain, discarding the liquid, and set aside.

In another saucepan, heat the oil and add the onion, bell pepper, and garlic. Sauté over medium heat for about 7 minutes. Stir in the catsup, molasses, Worcestershire sauce, and seasonings and cook for 3 minutes more, stirring frequently. Add the beans and potatoes, reduce the heat, and cook for about 15 minutes, stirring occasionally. Serve hot.

Yield: 4 to 6 servings

Each serving provides:

379		Calories	72	g	Carbohydrate
11	g	Protein	644	mg	Sodium
7	g	Fat	0	mg	Cholesterol
9	g	Dietary Fiber			

Chipotle Baked Campfire Beans

Cowboys subsisted on baked beans when out on the range, and smoked and cured meats provided much of the flavor. For this lean, modern version, I've replaced the bacon with chipotle peppers. Chipotles are large jalapeño peppers that have been dried and smoked. Chipotles are available canned or dried in most supermarkets.

1	cup dried navy or great northern beans, soaked and drained
2	chipotle peppers
2	tablespoons vegetable oil
1	medium onion, diced
2	cloves garlic, minced
2/3	cup catsup
1/3	cup molasses
1/3	cup brown sugar
2	tablespoons Worcestershire sauce
1/4	teaspoon ground black pepper
1/4	teaspoon salt

Place the beans and plenty of water to cover in a saucepan and cook over medium heat for 1 hour. Drain the beans, discarding the liquid, and set aside.

If the chipotle peppers are dried, soak them in warm water to cover for 30 minutes. Drain, remove the seeds, and mince.

Preheat the oven to 350°F.

In a flameproof casserole or Dutch oven, heat the oil and sauté the onion, garlic, and chiles for about 5 minutes. Stir in the catsup, molasses, brown sugar, Worcestershire sauce, black pepper, and salt and cook for 3 to 4 minutes more. Add the beans and blend well.

Cover the casserole dish and transfer to the oven. Bake for about 1 hour, stirring occasionally. Serve hot.

Yield: 4 servings

Each serving provides:

446	Calories	85	g	Carbohydrate
13	g Protein	721	mg	Sodium
8	g Fat	0	mg	Cholesterol
6	g Dietary Fiber			

Rum-Spiked Barbecued Baked Beans

Baked beans, mmm, mmm, good. Look up the term "comfort food" in the dictionary and you could find baked beans listed as an example. Baked beans nourish the spirit as well as the tummy.

Legend has it that Boston acquired the nickname "Beantown" because of the Bostonian propensity for baked beans and brown bread. Then, as now, baked beans were a hearty and thrifty meal. This slimmed down, jazzed up meatless version will leave you licking the plate. Rum provides a boost of feisty flavor.

½ cup dried navy or great northern beans,
　　soaked and drained
½ cup dried small red chili beans
　　or black beans, soaked and drained
2 tablespoons vegetable oil
1 medium onion, diced
2 cloves garlic, minced
½ cup catsup
½ cup dark rum
⅓ cup brown sugar
⅓ cup molasses
2 tablespoons Worcestershire sauce
½ teaspoon ground allspice
¼ teaspoon ground black pepper
¼ teaspoon salt

Place the beans and plenty of water to cover in a sauce-pan and cook over medium heat for about 1 hour. Drain the beans, discarding the liquid, and set aside. The beans will be slightly undercooked.

Preheat the oven to 350°F.

In a flameproof casserole or Dutch oven, heat the oil and sauté the onion and garlic for about 5 minutes. Stir in the catsup, rum, brown sugar, molasses, Worcestershire sauce, and seasonings and cook for 3 to 4 minutes more. Add the beans and blend well.

Cover the casserole dish and transfer to the oven. Bake for 1 hour, stirring occasionally. Serve hot with pumpernickel bread.

Yield: 4 servings

Each serving provides:

492	Calories	81 g	Carbohydrate
12 g	Protein	597 mg	Sodium
8 g	Fat	0 mg	Cholesterol
7 g	Dietary Fiber		

Rustic Well-Fried Beans
(Frijoles Refritos)

Well-fried beans is a more accurate translation of the term
frijoles refritos, *often called refried beans. The beans are
cooked, mashed, stirred, and cooked again, until finally they
exude the ultimate essence of bean-ness. Pinto beans are the
traditional bean for this dish, but you can also use black beans
or kidney beans.*

*Beans prepared in this fashion are versatile. Fill a warm
tortilla with beans, lettuce, tomatoes, and scallions, spoon a
little spicy salsa over it, and you have yourself a dandy
appetizer, light meal, or side dish.*

1   cup dried pinto, black, or red kidney beans,
      soaked and drained
2   tablespoons vegetable oil
1   medium onion, minced
½   jalapeño pepper, seeded and minced
1   teaspoon ground cumin
½   teaspoon salt
2   tablespoons minced fresh cilantro
½ to 2   teaspoons Tabasco
      or other bottled hot sauce

Place the beans in a saucepan, add plenty of water to cover, and cook for about 1 hour, until tender. Drain, reserving about ½ cup of the liquid, and set aside.

Heat the oil in a saucepan and add the onion. Sauté for about 5 to 7 minutes, until tender. Add the jalapeño, cumin, and salt and cook for 1 minute more.

Add half of the beans and a little of the reserved cooking liquid to the onion mixture and cook over medium heat. Mash the beans with a spoon, forming a coarse puree. Add more liquid as you mash the beans. Add the remaining beans and continue to mash the mixture. Cook for 15 to 20 minutes, and then stir in the cilantro and hot sauce. You can serve the beans now, or continue cooking over low heat, stirring frequently, until the beans form a thick pancake.

Yield: 2 cups

Each serving provides:

243	Calories	35	g	Carbohydrate
11 g	Protein	291	mg	Sodium
8 g	Fat	0	mg	Cholesterol
6 g	Dietary Fiber			

Madras Chick Peas
with Cauliflower

Cauliflower is matched well with nutty, chewy chick peas and a blend of earthy Indian curry flavors. Broccoflower, the hybridized broccoli and cauliflower vegetable, can also be used. One of this dish's integral flavors, garam masala, is actually a blend of Indian spices. Ground coriander may be substituted.

2 tablespoons vegetable oil
1 small onion, diced
1 large tomato, cored and chopped
2 cloves garlic, minced
½ tablespoon minced fresh ginger root
1 jalapeño or serrano pepper, seeded and minced
1 teaspoon garam masala
½ teaspoon ground turmeric
½ teaspoon ground cumin
½ teaspoon salt
¼ teaspoon ground coriander
2 cups cooked or canned chick peas, drained
2 cups cauliflower or broccoflower florets
1 cup water

Heat the oil in a skillet and add the onion, tomato, garlic, ginger, and jalapeño. Sauté for 5 to 7 minutes. Add the seasonings to the skillet and cook for 1 minute more, stirring frequently. Add the chick peas, cauliflower, and water and simmer for 25 to 30 minutes, stirring occasionally. Serve hot with rice and bread.

Yield: 4 servings

Each serving provides:

232	Calories	30 g	Carbohydrate
9 g	Protein	292 mg	Sodium
9 g	Fat	0 mg	Cholesterol
5 g	Dietary Fiber		

Cuban Black Beans and Rice

This is my version of the Cuban staple known as Moros y Christianos, *or Moors and Christians.*

For the beans:
1   cup dried black beans, soaked and drained
2½   cups water
1   hot chile pepper, seeded and minced (optional)
2   teaspoons ground cumin
2   teaspoons chili powder
1   teaspoon dried thyme
½   teaspoon ground black pepper
½   teaspoon salt

For the rice:
2   tablespoons vegetable oil
1   medium onion, diced
1   red or green bell pepper, seeded and diced
2   cloves garlic, minced
3   cups water
1½   cups uncooked white or brown rice

To make the beans, combine the beans, water, and seasonings (except the salt) in a saucepan. Cook over low heat for about 1 hour, stirring occasionally, until the beans are tender. Stir in the salt and set aside.

To make the rice, heat the oil in a saucepan and add the onion, pepper, and garlic. Sauté for 5 minutes. Add the water and rice, cover, and cook over medium heat for 15 minutes, until the rice is done. (If using brown rice, cook for 45 minutes.) Stir in the cooked beans and cook for a few minutes more. Remove from the heat and serve hot.

Yield: 4 servings

Each serving provides:

512	Calories	93	g	Carbohydrate
17	g Protein	296	mg	Sodium
8	g Fat	0	mg	Cholesterol
9	g Dietary Fiber			

Polenta with White Beans

Although polenta sounds like a dish listed on the social register of fine cuisine, it actually is a simple, down-to-earth cornmeal cake with roots in Italian cuisine. It is often served with herb-spiced white beans. In other parts of the world, versions of polenta are called coo coo, funghi, and just plain ol' corn mush. I think the name polenta is the best moniker.

For the polenta:
1	tablespoon vegetable or olive oil
2½	cups water
½	teaspoon salt
1	cup yellow cornmeal
¼	cup grated Parmesan cheese
2	tablespoons butter, melted

For the beans:
1	tablespoon vegetable oil
1	small onion, diced
2	cloves garlic, minced
2	cups cooked or canned cannellini or great northern beans, drained
2	tablespoons minced fresh chives
1	tablespoon fresh savory or thyme leaves
2	teaspoons dried oregano
¼	teaspoon ground black pepper
¼	teaspoon salt

To make the polenta, brush an 8½- by 4½-inch loaf pan with the oil.

Combine the water and salt in a saucepan and bring to a boil. Gradually stir in the cornmeal, cover, and cook for 12 to 15 minutes over low heat, until the polenta is thick and soft.

Stir in the Parmesan cheese and melted butter, then spoon the polenta into the oiled pan. Allow the polenta to cool to room temperature. Wrap and chill for 1 hour before reheating.

To make the beans, heat the oil in a saucepan and add the onion and garlic. Sauté for 5 to 7 minutes. Add the beans, herbs, and seasonings and cook for 10 to 15 minutes over medium heat, stirring occasionally. Keep warm.

To reheat the polenta, invert it onto a flat surface and cut into 4 pieces. Place the polenta pieces into a lightly oiled skillet and cook for 4 to 5 minutes on each side. Transfer the polenta to serving plates and serve with the beans on the side.

Yield: 4 servings

Each serving provides:

381	Calories	49 g	Carbohydrate
13 g	Protein	564 mg	Sodium
15 g	Fat	19 mg	Cholesterol
5 g	Dietary Fiber		

Red Chili Beans
and Couscous

Couscous, the tiny grain-shaped pasta, is so very, very easy to prepare: Simply combine it with boiling water and let sit for about 10 minutes. By mixing couscous with small red chili beans, you get a fast micro-version of Red Beans and Brown Rice (page 190).

2   tablespoons vegetable oil
1   small onion, diced
1   small red or green bell pepper, seeded and diced
2   cloves garlic, minced
1   jalapeño pepper, seeded and minced (optional)
2   cups cooked or canned small red chili beans
     or black beans, drained
1   cup boiling water
1   teaspoon chili powder
½ to 2   teaspoons Tabasco
     or other bottled hot sauce
½   teaspoon ground black pepper
½   teaspoon salt
1   cup uncooked couscous

Heat the oil in a saucepan and add the onion, bell pepper, garlic, and jalapeño. Sauté for about 7 minutes. Add the beans, water, and seasonings and simmer for about 10 minutes over medium heat. Stir in the couscous, cover the pan, and turn off the heat. Let stand on the stove for 10 minutes.

Fluff the couscous and beans and serve at once.

Yield: 4 servings

Each serving provides:

366	Calories	60 g	Carbohydrate
14 g	Protein	297 mg	Sodium
8 g	Fat	0 mg	Cholesterol
4 g	Dietary Fiber		

Spiced Aromatic Lentils with Cucumber Raita

Raita, an Indian condiment that soothes the tongue, is a cooling blend of yogurt, cucumber, and spices. Raita is a nice accompaniment to most spicy dishes, and is ideally juxtaposed with this fragrantly spiced lentil dish.

For the lentils:

1½	cups red or brown lentils, rinsed
4	cups water
½	teaspoon ground turmeric
1½	tablespoons vegetable oil
1	medium onion, finely chopped
2	cloves garlic, minced
½	teaspoon ground cumin
½	teaspoon ground coriander
½	teaspoon salt
¼	teaspoon ground cayenne pepper
1	tablespoon minced fresh cilantro

For the raita:

1½	cups plain lowfat yogurt
1	cup finely chopped cucumber (do not peel)
½	teaspoon paprika
¼	teaspoon salt

Place the lentils, water, and turmeric in a saucepan and cook over low heat for 45 minutes, until tender. Drain any excess water.

Meanwhile, combine all of the raita ingredients in a mixing bowl, cover, and chill until ready to serve.

When the lentils are almost done, heat the oil in another saucepan and add the onion and garlic. Sauté for 5 minutes. Stir in the seasonings (except the cilantro) and cook 1 minute more. Stir in the lentils and cilantro and simmer for 5 to 7 minutes.

Serve the lentils with the cucumber raita spooned over the top.

Yield: 4 servings

Each serving provides:

367	Calories	53	g	Carbohydrate
25	g Protein	478	mg	Sodium
7	g Fat	5	mg	Cholesterol
9	g Dietary Fiber			

Sweet Plantains
with Ground Nut Sauce

Long before there was processed peanut butter, there was ground nut sauce, a popular African condiment. Both ground nuts (peanuts) and plantains (also known as vegetable bananas or platanos) are grown in the tropical regions of the world, and they form a natural taste alliance. Sweet yellow plantains taste like a cross between a banana and a potato. They're a great side dish.

For the sauce:
1 tablespoon vegetable oil
1 small onion, finely chopped
½ cayenne or other red chile pepper,
   seeded and minced
1 tablespoon minced fresh ginger root
1 cup chunky peanut butter
¾ cup water
2 tablespoons tomato puree
1 teaspoon dried thyme
½ teaspoon salt

2 tablespoons butter or oil
3 or 4 ripe yellow plantains, peeled
   and sliced ¼ inch thick

To make the sauce, heat the oil in a saucepan and add the onion, chile, and ginger. Sauté for 5 to 7 minutes. Blend in the peanut butter, water, tomato puree, and seasonings. Cook over low heat for 5 to 10 minutes, stirring frequently. Transfer to a serving bowl and keep warm.

Heat the butter in a skillet. Place the plantains in the skillet and cook over medium heat until each side is golden brown, about 7 minutes. Turn the plantains every few minutes. Transfer to plates and spoon the ground nut sauce over the top.

Yield: 4 servings

Each serving provides:

669	Calories	68	g	Carbohydrate
18	g Protein	684	mg	Sodium
42	g Fat	16	mg	Cholesterol
7	g Dietary Fiber			

Ancho Chile–Tinged Beans

Ancho chiles are dried poblano peppers. They are large, anvil-shaped peppers with a deep mahogany color and fruity flavor. They are extremely popular in Mexico, where they are used in a variety of sauces, including mole sauce. Here they infuse beans with a dash of sparkling heat. This is great way to perk up leftover beans.

1   ancho chile pepper
2   tablespoons vegetable oil
1   small onion, finely chopped
2 or 3   scallions, finely chopped
2   cloves garlic, minced
2   cups cooked or canned red kidney beans,
      black beans, or white lima beans, drained
½   teaspoon ground cumin
½   teaspoon salt

Soak the ancho chile in warm water for about 1 hour. Drain, discarding the liquid. Remove the seeds and mince the chile.

Heat the oil in a saucepan and add the onion, scallions, garlic, and chile. Sauté for about 5 minutes. Add the beans and seasonings and cook for about 10 minutes over medium heat, stirring occasionally.

Serve as a side dish with rice or pasta.

Yield: 2 servings

Each serving provides:

402		Calories	52 g	Carbohydrate
17	g	Protein	559 mg	Sodium
16	g	Fat	0 mg	Cholesterol
8	g	Dietary Fiber		

Island Rice Pudding with Adzuki Beans

This is a tropical-inspired adaptation of the classic dessert of leftover rice. The bananas add an enticing new dimension.

3 cups cooked short-grain rice
2 cups milk or light cream
1 cup cooked or canned adzuki beans, drained
½ cup sugar
½ cup raisins
¼ cup dark rum
¾ teaspoon ground nutmeg
2 bananas, peeled and mashed

Combine all of the ingredients in a saucepan and cook for 15 minutes over low heat, stirring frequently. Transfer the pudding to a bowl and chill for at least 1 hour before serving.

When you are ready to serve the pudding, spoon it into bowls and garnish with a sprig of mint and a dusting of nutmeg.

Yield: 6 servings

Each serving provides:

377	Calories	75 g	Carbohydrate
8 g	Protein	43 mg	Sodium
3 g	Fat	11 mg	Cholesterol
2 g	Dietary Fiber		

Sweet Adzuki Beans

When sweetened with sugar, the natural nutty flavor of adzuki beans is intensified, making them a tasty ingredient for cakes, breads, pancakes, and puddings. These beans can also be spooned over waffles, yogurt, or ice cream. Traditional Asian recipes call for the beans to be mashed into a paste and used as filling for spongelike rolls and cakes. Try them as a filling the next time you make pastries.

1 cup dried adzuki beans, soaked and drained
4 cups water
½ cup sugar

Place the beans and water in a saucepan and cook over medium heat for 1 to 1½ hours, until tender. Stir in the sugar and cook for 10 minutes more, stirring frequently. To thicken, mash the beans against the side of the pan with a wooden spoon.

Remove from the heat and chill until ready to use.

Yield: about 2 cups

Each serving provides:

276 Calories
12 g Protein
1 g Fat
5 g Dietary Fiber

57 g Carbohydrate
8 mg Sodium
0 mg Cholesterol

Beans for Beginners

Here's a quick and easy recipe for folks getting to know beans for the first time, or simply reacquainting themselves with the legume family. Serve over rice and you've got yourself a nice side dish.

2 tablespoons vegetable oil
1 small onion, diced
1 small red or green bell pepper, seeded and diced
2 cloves garlic, minced
1 jalapeño pepper, seeded and minced (optional)
2 cups canned black beans
   or small red chili beans, drained
1 teaspoon ground cumin
½ to 1 teaspoon Tabasco or other bottled hot sauce
¼ teaspoon ground black pepper
¼ teaspoon salt

Heat the oil in a saucepan and add the onion, bell pepper, garlic, and jalapeño. Sauté for about 7 minutes. Add the beans and seasonings and cook for 10 to 15 minutes over medium heat, stirring occasionally.

Serve as a side dish with rice.

Yield: 2 servings

Each serving provides:

306	Calories	42 g	Carbohydrate
14 g	Protein	313 mg	Sodium
14 g	Fat	0 mg	Cholesterol
13 g	Dietary Fiber		

Succotash with Purple Kale

Succotash is a traditional native American dish of lima beans and corn. I've added purple kale, also called salad savoy or flowering kale. It makes for a picturesque and healthful side dish.

2   cups frozen Green Fordhook lima beans
1   tablespoon vegetable oil
1   medium onion, diced
2   cups corn kernels, fresh, frozen, or canned
1   cup coarsely chopped purple kale or green kale
¼   teaspoon ground black pepper
¼   teaspoon salt

Place the lima beans in boiling water to cover and cook for 8 to 10 minutes, until tender. Drain, discarding the liquid.

Heat the oil in a saucepan and add the onion. Sauté for 4 minutes, then add the beans, corn, kale, and seasonings. Cook for about 5 minutes, stirring occasionally. Transfer to serving bowls and serve at once.

Yield: 4 servings

Each serving provides:

103	Calories	18	g	Carbohydrate
4	g Protein	101	mg	Sodium
2	g Fat	0	mg	Cholesterol
7	g Dietary Fiber			

Beans
for Breakfast

Beans in the morning. I know what you're thinking: Coffee beans, maybe, but the kind of beans I'm talking about, maybe not. Okay, that's cool. You may not think of beans as the quintessential breakfast fare, but perhaps this chapter will change your perception.

Let's cut to the chase: Black Bean–Cumin Crêpes, Pink Bean and Sweet Potato Hash Browns, Emily's Squash and Adzuki Bean Pancakes, Sizzlin' Southwestern Omelet, and Breakfast Bean Burrito with Havarti Cheese are some of the enjoyable breakfast entrees you'll find here. These breakfast dishes are artfully flavored with beans and far from overpowering.

Even if preparing an elaborate breakfast is not in the cards for you, there is always brunch. Most of the recipes in this chapter make ideal brunch items. When the time comes for a special morning spread any day of the week, this chapter makes it easy to include beans in the menu. Eggs play a prominent role here, but egg substitutes may be used.

Breakfast is one of my favorite meals. I never miss it, no matter how hectic the morning is. Breakfast gives me sustenance and energy for the day to come, and allows me to collect my thoughts over a cup of coffee in a calm environment (most of the time). Wholesome beans are a welcome ingredient in many of my favorite breakfast dishes.

The theme of this chapter is moderation, of course. I may be a self-proclaimed spokesperson for beans, but in the words of Clint Eastwood, a man's got to know his limitations. I won't be adding beans to my cereal anytime in the near future.

Black Bean–Cumin Crêpes

Crêpes are slimmed-down pancakes. For eons, crêpes came in only one flavor—plain—and were typically served with an industrial-strength white sauce. My version incorporates black beans and cumin into the batter, and the result is a tasty and satisfying detour from tradition. This is a great brunch item, especially when served with fresh tomato salsa.

Some crêpe-making tips: Start with a hot pan, and flip with one smooth, fluid motion. Write off the first crêpe—its job is to season the pan, so don't be discouraged if it looks decidedly uncrêpe-like. Keep your chin up and try again.

2	eggs, beaten
1	cup all-purpose flour
1¼	cups milk
¼	teaspoon salt
1	tablespoon ground cumin
⅛	teaspoon ground cayenne pepper
3 to 4	tablespoons melted butter
1	cup cooked or canned black beans, drained and pureed
2	tomatoes, cored and diced
2	ripe avocadoes, peeled, pitted, and sliced
4 to 6	scallions, finely chopped
1	cup light sour cream or lowfat yogurt

Combine the eggs, flour, milk, salt, cumin, and cayenne in a large mixing bowl. Fold in the butter and pureed beans and refrigerate the batter for 15 to 30 minutes.

Heat a lightly greased 8-inch crêpe pan or skillet and ladle about ½ cup of batter into the pan. Tilt the pan to ease the batter around the base, forming a thin, round pancake. When the edges of the crêpe are golden brown, flip the crêpe with a smooth motion. Continue cooking until the remaining surface is golden brown and then remove to a warm plate.

Cook the remaining batter in the same fashion, adding about a teaspoon of oil to the pan after cooking each crêpe.

To fill the crêpes, place them on a serving plate and spoon equal portions of the tomatoes, avocados, scallions, and sour cream onto half of each crêpe. Wrap the crêpe around the filling, burrito style, and roll tight. Serve hot with salsa.

Yield: 4 to 6 servings

Each serving provides:

568	Calories	43 g	Carbohydrate
16 g	Protein	263 mg	Sodium
39 g	Fat	131 mg	Cholesterol
4 g	Dietary Fiber		

Emily's Squash and Adzuki Bean Pancakes

My friend Emily prepares an autumn feast of squash pancakes, apple chutney, and drop-dead strong coffee. Nutty adzuki beans are a natural ingredient for these deep orange pancakes, and fragrant nutmeg and allspice coax out the mild but ambitious flavor of squash. As with crêpes, keep your chin up and flip with one smooth motion. (Emily has even mastered the art of flipping the pancakes with a flick of her wrist, but she loses one every once in a while.)

2	cups uncooked, peeled, diced acorn or butternut squash or 1½ cups canned, mashed pumpkin
1½	cups cooked or canned adzuki beans, drained
1½	cups all-purpose flour
¼	cup brown sugar
2	teaspoons baking powder
1	teaspoon salt
2	large eggs, beaten
1¾	cups buttermilk or milk
¼	cup melted butter
½	teaspoon ground allspice
½	teaspoon ground nutmeg

Place the squash in boiling water to cover and cook for 12 to 15 minutes, until soft. Drain and cool. Transfer to a mixing bowl and mash the squash with the beans.

Combine the dry ingredients in a mixing bowl. In a separate bowl, whisk the eggs, buttermilk, and butter together. Fold the liquid ingredients into the dry ingredients. Blend in the squash-bean mixture along with the allspice and nutmeg.

Preheat a lightly greased griddle or skillet. When the surface is sizzling, spoon about ½ cup of the batter onto the griddle, forming a round pancake. Flip after 3 to 4 minutes, or when the edges are golden brown. Continue cooking until the other side of the pancake is golden brown. Remove the pancake to a serving plate and repeat the process with the remaining batter. Cover the finished pancakes with waxed paper.

Serve the pancakes with apple chutney or apple butter and a strong morning beverage.

Yield: 8 pancakes

Each serving provides:

278	Calories	39 g	Carbohydrate
9 g	Protein	533 mg	Sodium
10 g	Fat	71 mg	Cholesterol
3 g	Dietary Fiber		

Variation:
Emily likes to substitute whole wheat flour for half of the all-purpose flour. She also adds raisins, walnuts, and granola, depending on her mood.

Sizzlin' Southwestern Omelet

This is a brunch-size omelet, bursting at the seams. The flavors of the American Southwest—peppers, corn and black beans, cumin and cilantro—will wake up your taste buds with exuberant style. Constructing the perfect omelet requires a little preparation, the freshest ingredients, an eye for aesthetics, and, more than anything, a large, nonstick cooking skillet.

½   cup cooked or canned black beans, drained
¼   cup corn kernels, fresh, frozen, or canned
¼   cup minced red or green bell pepper
¼   cup diced tomato
2   tablespoons minced fresh chives or scallions
2   tablespoons minced fresh cilantro
1 to 2   teaspoons seeded, minced jalapeño pepper
½   teaspoon ground cumin
6   eggs, beaten
2   tablespoons milk
1½   tablespoons vegetable oil
½   cup shredded Monterey jack, provolone,
        or Colby cheese

Combine the black beans, corn, bell pepper, tomato, herbs, jalapeño, and cumin in a mixing bowl. Set aside. In another mixing bowl, whisk the eggs with the milk. Heat about 1 tablespoon of the oil in a 9-inch omelet pan or well-seasoned skillet. Cook over moderately high heat for about 30 seconds or until the oil sizzles.

Add about half the beaten eggs to the skillet. Swirl to the edges of the pan. Reduce the heat and cook for 1 to 2 minutes; then slide a spatula underneath the omelet to ease the excess uncooked egg mixture onto the pan's surface.

When the omelet is light brown around the edge and the top surface is barely moist, place half of the bean mixture on one half of the omelet. Sprinkle ¼ cup of the shredded cheese on top of the mixture and gently fold the other half of the omelet over the mixture, forming a half-moon. Cover the pan and cook for about 1 minute more; then turn off the heat. Let the omelet sit in the pan for another minute and then slide it onto a warm plate.

Re-season the pan with the remaining oil and repeat the process. Serve the omelets with salsa, guacamole, roasted potatoes, and warmed flour tortillas.

Yield: 2 large omelets (3 or 4 servings)

Each serving provides:

257	Calories	9 g	Carbohydrate
16 g	Protein	178 mg	Sodium
17 g	Fat	335 mg	Cholesterol
1 g	Dietary Fiber		

Breakfast Bean Burrito
with Havarti Cheese

Take your favorite scrambled egg creation, wrap it in a flour tortilla, and you have a breakfast burrito. This is my favorite combination with black beans or red chili beans. The creamy texture and flavor of Havarti cheese meld the warm flavors together.

1   tablespoon vegetable oil or butter
1   red bell pepper, seeded and diced
8   mushrooms, sliced
4   scallions, chopped
1   jalapeño or serrano pepper, seeded and minced
    (optional)
1   cup cooked or canned red chili beans
    or black beans, drained
½   cup corn kernels, fresh, frozen, or canned
1   teaspoon ground cumin
½   teaspoon ground black pepper
¼   teaspoon salt
6   eggs, beaten
1   cup shredded Havarti cheese
4   (10-inch) flour tortillas

In a large, nonstick skillet, heat the oil and add the bell pepper, mushrooms, scallions, and jalapeño. Sauté for 5 to 7 minutes, until soft. Stir in the beans, corn, and seasonings and cook for 2 to 3 minutes more. Whisk in the eggs and cook over medium heat, stirring frequently. When the eggs are completely cooked (fluffy, not brown), remove from the heat and fold in the cheese.

Warm the tortillas over a burner or hot pan and then place on plates. Spoon the egg-bean mixture into the centers, forming logs. Roll the tortilla around the mixture and serve with tomato salsa.

Yield: 4 servings

Each serving provides:

512	Calories	50 g	Carbohydrate
27 g	Protein	714 mg	Sodium
23 g	Fat	347 mg	Cholesterol
4 g	Dietary Fiber		

Egyptian Ful Medames

My aunt Margie, who has visited Egypt many times in her life, introduced me to ful medames, *the Egyptian national dish. Ful medames is served everywhere in Egypt, from street vendors to elegant restaurants. Traditionally, the beans are "buried" beneath the eggs and spices. The fava beans in Egypt are smaller than European fava beans and more globe shaped. They are available in the specialty section of supermarkets.*

2 cups cooked or canned small fava beans
1 teaspoon ground cumin
2 cloves garlic, minced
4 hard-boiled eggs
1 tablespoon minced fresh parsley
1 lemon, quartered
¼ cup olive oil
Salt and ground black pepper, to taste

Heat the beans in a saucepan until steaming, stirring occasionally. Stir in the cumin and garlic. Divide the beans among 4 soup bowls.

Place a hard-boiled egg on top of each bowl of beans. "Bury the beans" by mashing the eggs into the beans. Sprinkle parsley over the mixture and then squeeze a wedge of lemon over each bowl. Drizzle 1 tablespoon of oil over each dish, season with salt and pepper to taste, and serve at once.

Yield: 4 servings

Each serving provides:

306	Calories	22 g	Carbohydrate
14 g	Protein	69 mg	Sodium
19 g	Fat	213 mg	Cholesterol
5 g	Dietary Fiber		

Sweet Potato Frittata
with Green Lima Beans

Frittata is a hearty Italian potato-and-egg dish. This version is enhanced with green lima beans. It is designed for the luxurious pace of brunch. Although white potatoes are traditionally used, I prefer the change of pace that sweet potatoes offer. Don't peel the potatoes; the skins have valuable nutrients and flavor.

2	tablespoons vegetable oil
2	cups diced sweet potatoes
6	mushrooms, sliced
4	scallions, chopped
1	green bell pepper, seeded and diced
1	cup diced zucchini
2	cloves garlic, minced
1½	cups frozen Green Fordhook lima beans
1	cup corn kernels, fresh, frozen, or canned
1	teaspoon paprika
1	teaspoon dried thyme
½	teaspoon salt
¼	teaspoon ground cayenne pepper
6	eggs, beaten
1	cup grated Monterey jack or Havarti cheese

Place the lima beans in boiling water to cover and cook for 8 minutes. Drain, discarding the liquid, and set aside.

In a large, nonstick skillet or Dutch oven, heat the oil and add the sweet potatoes. Sauté for about 10 minutes, until easily pierced with a fork. Add the mushrooms, scallions, bell pepper, zucchini, and garlic and cook for about 7 minutes more, stirring occasionally. Stir in the lima beans, corn, and seasonings and cook for 3 to 5 minutes.

Reduce the heat and pour the eggs into the pan, blending them into the vegetables. Sprinkle the cheese over the top and cover the pan. Cook for 1 to 2 minutes more and then turn off the heat. Let stand for 5 minutes.

Serve with whole wheat toast or English muffins. Pass the hot sauce at the table, natch.

Yield: 4 servings

Each serving provides:

471	Calories	42 g	Carbohydrate
24 g	Protein	575 mg	Sodium
24 g	Fat	349 mg	Cholesterol
12 g	Dietary Fiber		

Variation:
Replace the 3 eggs with 3 egg whites, or try an egg substitute.

Pink Bean and Sweet Potato Hash Browns

Originally, this was going to be a bean cake, but it went awry. The ingredients didn't quite hold together. But you know, I couldn't stop eating the result. I had stumbled upon a very satisfying breakfast dish. It doesn't have a namby-pamby artistic presentation, but it is hearty and tasty.

2	cups diced sweet potatoes (do not peel)
1½	tablespoons vegetable oil
1	small onion, diced
2	cloves garlic, minced
1	jalapeño pepper, seeded and minced (optional)
2	cups cooked or canned pink beans
	or small red chili beans, drained
2	tablespoons minced fresh parsley
1	teaspoon ground cumin
1	teaspoon paprika
1 to 2	teaspoons Tabasco
	or other bottled hot sauce
½	teaspoon salt
¼	teaspoon ground cayenne pepper

Place the sweet potatoes in boiling water to cover and cook for about 15 minutes, until tender. Drain in a colander and cool slightly under cold running water. Heat the oil in a saucepan and add the onion, garlic, and jalapeño. Sauté for about 5 minutes. Stir in the sweet potatoes, beans, and seasonings and cook for 7 to 10 minutes over low heat, stirring frequently. Fluff the mixture and serve hot.

Yield: 4 servings

Each serving provides:

302	Calories	51 g	Carbohydrate
12 g	Protein	300 mg	Sodium
6 g	Fat	0 mg	Cholesterol
8 g	Dietary Fiber		

White Bean
and Corn Risotto
Skillet Cakes

*Here's a swell morning dish to give you energy for the day
ahead.*

*It's also a splendid use for leftover arborio rice or risotto.
Arborio rice is quite glutinous, and adapts well to the
batterlike consistency required for a skillet cake. The beans
and corn provide the necessary sustenance.*

2 cups cooked arborio rice
2 eggs, beaten
2 cups cooked or canned navy
    or great northern beans, drained
1 cup corn kernels, fresh, frozen, or canned
¼ cup grated Parmesan cheese
2 scallions, finely chopped
2 tablespoons minced fresh cilantro or parsley
2 tablespoons bread crumbs
¼ teaspoon salt
¼ teaspoon ground cayenne pepper

Combine all of the ingredients in a mixing bowl and blend thoroughly. Mash the mixture against the side of the bowl.

Heat a lightly greased skillet (preferably nonstick) over medium heat and ladle about ½ cup of the mixture into the pan. Spread the batter out, forming a pancake. Cook for about 5 minutes, until the edges are golden brown. Gently flip the cake and finish cooking the other side.

Slide the cake onto a serving plate and repeat the process with the remaining mixture. Add 1 teaspoon of oil to the pan before cooking if the cake sticks to the pan. Cover the finished cakes with waxed paper until ready to serve. Serve with salsa or light sour cream.

Yield: 4 servings

Each serving provides:

412	Calories	64 g	Carbohydrate
17 g	Protein	297 mg	Sodium
10 g	Fat	110 mg	Cholesterol
5 g	Dietary Fiber		

Pinto Bean
and Double Corn Bread

It took me years to develop a good corn bread recipe. So many recipes are dry, crumbly, and uninspiring. This version hits the spot. The alliance of beans and corn once again yields a satisfying result. Although this corn bread makes a scrumptious breakfast, it is also a tasty companion to soup, chili, or stew.

2	cups yellow cornmeal
2	cups all-purpose flour
½	cup sugar
2	tablespoons baking powder
1	teaspoon salt
4	eggs, beaten
1	cup buttermilk
1	cup milk
½	cup melted butter
1	cup cooked or canned pinto beans
	or black beans, drained
1	cup corn kernels, fresh, frozen, or canned

Preheat the oven to 375°F.

Place the cornmeal, flour, sugar, baking powder, and salt in a mixing bowl and blend together. In a separate bowl, whisk together the eggs, buttermilk, milk, and melted butter. Gently fold the liquid ingredients into the dry ingredients until the mixture forms a batter. Fold in the beans and corn. Pour the batter into a greased 9- by 13-inch baking pan.

Bake for 20 to 25 minutes, until the crust is lightly browned and a toothpick inserted in the center comes out clean. Remove from the heat and let cool for a few minutes. Cut into squares and serve warm.

Yield: 12 servings

Each serving provides:

341	Calories	51 g	Carbohydrate
9 g	Protein	561 mg	Sodium
11 g	Fat	95 mg	Cholesterol
3 g	Dietary Fiber		

Pumpkin Hominy Muffins
with Adzuki Beans

*Once upon a time I owned a muffin shop. I had many
moments to contemplate all of the different varieties of muffins
in the universe. I am not sure what inspired this combination,
but it proved to be a winner. It has a flat appearance, like an
English muffin.*

1	cup canned hominy, drained
1	cup cooked or canned adzuki beans, drained
½	cup butter, softened
½	cup brown sugar, firmly packed
½	cup granulated sugar
2	eggs
1½	cups cooked, mashed pumpkin
½	cup buttermilk
2	cups unbleached flour
1	tablespoon baking powder
1	teaspoon salt
1	teaspoon ground cinnamon
½	teaspoon ground nutmeg or allspice
½	teaspoon baking soda

Preheat the oven to 375°F.

Place the hominy and beans into a food processor fitted with a steel blade and process for 10 seconds. Set aside.

In a mixing bowl, blend the butter and sugars until creamy. Beat in the eggs one at a time, until the mixture is fluffy. Blend in the hominy mixture, pumpkin, and buttermilk and mix well.

Mix the dry ingredients in a separate bowl and then gently fold into pumpkin batter. Scoop the batter into large, greased muffin tins.

Bake for about 20 minutes or until a toothpick inserted in the center of the muffins comes out clean. Remove from the pan after 10 minutes and let cool on a rack.

Yield: 10 to 12 large muffins

Each serving provides:

297	Calories	45	g	Carbohydrate
6	g Protein	534	mg	Sodium
11	g Fat	62	mg	Cholesterol
2	g Dietary Fiber			

Index

pudding with adzuki beans, 214
wild, vegetable paella, with
fava beans, 158–159
Risotto
skillet cakes, white bean and corn,
234–235
vegetable, with cranberry beans,
140–141
white bean and sun-dried tomato,
138–139
Rocky Mountain Chili with
Anasazi Beans, 32
Roman beans. *See* Cranberry beans
Roti, stuffed with curried chick pea
filling, 150–151
Roughage in beans, 4
Roux, 34, 35
Rum-Spiked Barbecued Baked Beans,
196–197
Rustic Well-Fried Beans (Frijoles
Refritos), 198–199
Rutabagas, stew, split pea and barley,
40–41

Saint Lucian Pumpkin and White Bean
Soup, 36–37
Salads, 68–102
about, 68–69
beet, potato, and large bean, 92–93
black bean, beet, and jicama, 76–77
black-eyed pea, with pasta wheels and
asparagus, 86–87
Bolivian bean, 102
ceci bean and pasta, Sicilian, 80–81
cooking beans for, 69
couscous and lentil, Mediterranean,
72–73
island heat, with spinach, goat cheese,
and red beans, 98–99
lentil and couscous, Southwestern,
94–95
lentil, apple, and bow tie pasta, 96–97
lima bean and kohlrabi, with
Szechuan peanut sauce, 78–79
pasta and red bean, with pesto,
100–101
spa bean, with balsamic-basil
vinaigrette, 90–91
tabooley with chick peas, 84–85
three-bean, with Greek flavors, 82–83
two-bean, with mint tahini sauce,
88–89

warm quinoa, corn, and cranberry
bean, 74–75
wheat garden, 84–85
white bean and sweet potato, 70–71
Salsa, piquant black bean and red
tomato, 116–117
Salt, 3–4, 6
Sambar, Sri Lankan, with
coconut-cilantro chutney, 176–177
Sauces. *See also* Dipping sauces
coconut-cilantro chutney, 176–177
mint tahini, 88–89
peanut, African, 210–211
pesto, 100–101
skordalia, 114–115
Szechuan peanut, 78–79
Sauté, summer, with pattypan squash,
Swiss chard, and red beans, 142–143
Scotch bonnet pepper–black bean sauce,
124–125
Seasoning, 6–7, 8
Shelly beans. *See* Cranberry beans
Sicilian Ceci Bean and Pasta Salad, 80–81
Side dishes, 182–217
about, 182–183
ancho chile–tinged beans, 212–213
baked beans, 194–197
beginners' beans, 216
black beans and rice, Cuban, 202–203
chick peas with cauliflower, Madras,
200–201
plaintains with peanut sauce, 210–211
polenta with white beans, 204–205
pumpkin rice with gungo peas,
188–189
red beans and brown rice, 190–191
red chili beans and couscous, 206–207
rice and peas, Caribbean, 186–187
rice pudding, island, with adzuki
beans, 214
spiced aromatic lentils with cucumber
raita, 208–209
stovetop beans with sweet potatoes,
192–193
succotash, 184–185, 217
sweet adzuki beans, 215
well-fried beans, 198–199
Sizzlin' Southwestern Omelet, 224–225
Skillet cakes, white bean and corn
risotto, 234–235
Skordalia sauce, 114–115
Small dishes. *See* Appetizers; Side dishes